MYSTIC ALASKA

BY

KAREN J SIMON

MYSTIC ALASKA

By Karen J Simon

Revised ©2020
©2014

Front cover photo by Karen J Simon
Back cover original painting by Karen J Simon
Photos, paintings and poetry by Karen J Simon

Published by Create Space

ISBN numbers:
ISBN-13: 978-1502947109
ISBN -10: 1502947102

TABLE OF CONTENTS

Welcome to Alaska……………………………………………………..1

Alaska's Symbols…………………..………………………………3

The Last Ice Age……………………………………………………4

Alaska…………………………………………………...6

Remnants of the Ice Age……………………………………8

Glaciers……………………………………………………...9

Patterns in the Ice……………………………………14

Northern Lights……………………………………………14

The Lights of Heaven…………………………………..........17

Northern Lights Over Alaska…………………………19

Ice Fog………………………………………………...21

Winter Wonderland……………………………………...22

Rainbows……………………………………………...24

Waterfalls………………………………………………...27

Alaska Sunrise……………………………………......…..30

Alaska Sunset……………………………………………31

Alaska Wildlife…………………………………………...32

Whale Watching…………………………………………34

Bird Watching……………………………………………36

Alaska Flowers……………………………………………38

Winter Driving……………………………………......…….40

Welcome to Alaska

Alaska has captured the imagination of the world since it was first discovered. There is something in the name, something in the location of the land, something in its history, in its remoteness and untamed, mostly unpeopled wilderness that holds an unwavering curiosity to see it, to experience it – if only very briefly.

I have always found it amusing when people answer the question, "Have you ever been to Alaska?" with the response, "Yes, I took a cruise up there."

"Did you go inland?" I ask.

"No, we just cruised."

If you have only cruised the Inside Passage, you have never been to Alaska. That's like a European saying, "Yes, I've been to America. I cruised the Gulf of Mexico." Or an American saying, "Yes, I've been to Europe. I cruised the Mediterranean."

A few years ago I had the pleasure of having breakfast with a pastor from the lower 48. It was his 11th year coming to Alaska to do a Christmas service in a remote Alaska village.

"So you've been to Fairbanks?" I asked.

"No. I have a friend who lives near Anchorage and he told me there was nothing north of Denali."

Alaska is much bigger than the Inland Passage and extends far beyond the city limits of Anchorage. It is a vast land that remained virtually unexplored until the Alcan Highway opened it to the outside world following WWII. The development of oil fields on the North Slope of Alaska opened the land even more bringing thousands of people to the state. Some hated it and left. Some fell in love and refused to leave.

Alaska has more coastline than the entire lower 48 states combined. It is twice the size of Texas unless, of course, the tide is out and then it is three times bigger. You could take the three largest states – Texas, California and Montana – set them into Alaska and still have room left over for Rhode Island. Consider the total population of those states combined. Fort Worth, Texas, by itself, has a larger population than the entire state of Alaska. The largest number of Alaska residents live in the greater Anchorage area, leaving the rest of the state virtually unpopulated.

So if you've never REALLY been to Alaska, don't feel alone, there are a good number of Alaskans who have seen far less of the state than most tourists.

Can you see Russia from Alaska? Of course you can! Fifty five miles across the Bering Strait from Cape Prince of Wales in Alaska, East Cape, Siberia (Russia) is a thin line on the horizon. Halfway between the capes are two islands separated by 2.3 miles of water. Big Diomede is owned by Russia, Little Diomede is part of Alaska.

The photos in this book were not taken by a professional photographer, they were taken by a resident tourist. This is the Alaska I called home for over 50 years. This is the Alaska that I have come to love.

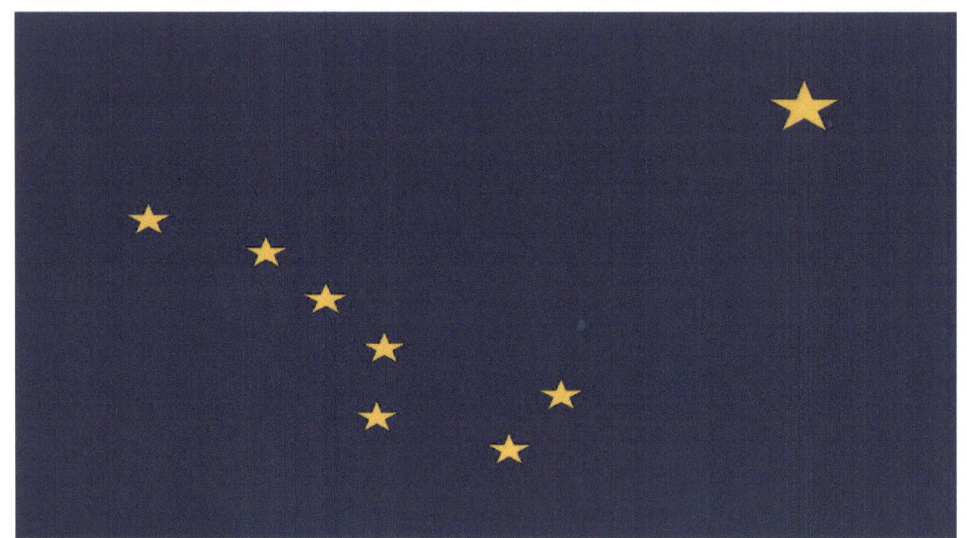

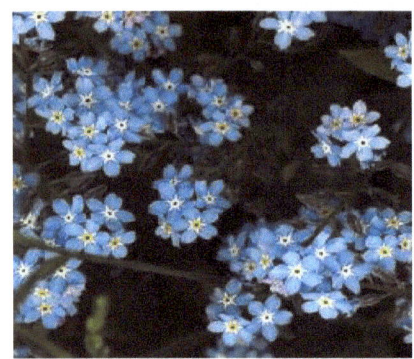

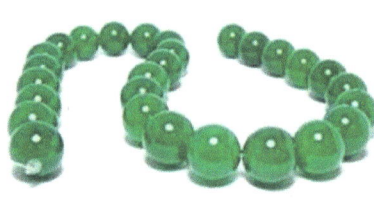

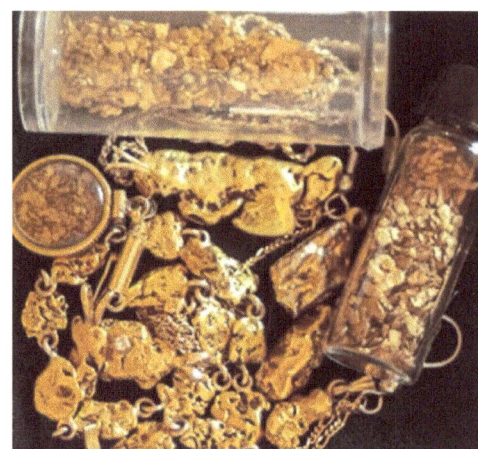

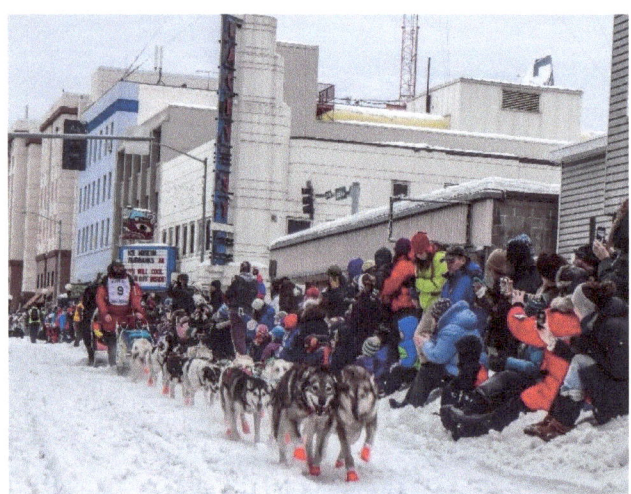

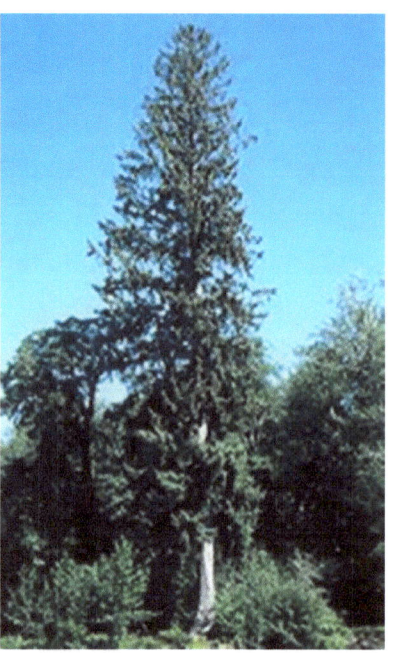

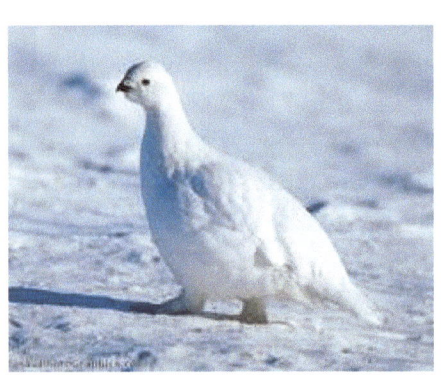

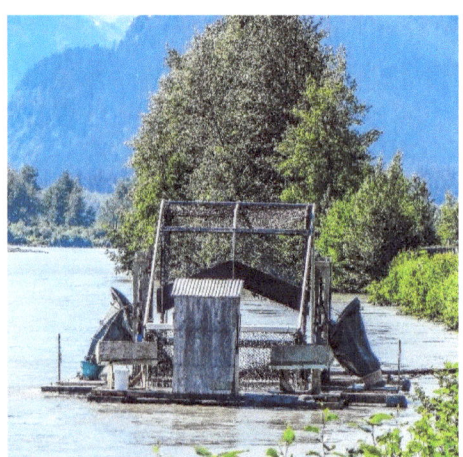

ALASKA'S SYMBOLS

Nations and states for many a year

Have chosen symbols to hold especially dear.

Alaska was no exception to the rule.

In 1926, the Alaska American Legion turned to students in school

To design the flag that would wave o'er the state.

Of 142 entries, that of Benny Benson was chosen first rate.

The state song reflects some of the words he wrote

In the wonders of which it chose to take note.

Was the choice of the Forget-Me-Not more than two fold

With its name, soft blue color and a heart of gold?

Gold, it was, that brought Alaska great fame

As the state's official mineral it well earned its name.

In winters long ago, dog sled was the method of transport,

Dog mushing now is the state's official sport.

The Willow Ptarmigan is a bird hard to sight

when it dons its garment of winter white.

King Salmon, to fisherman's delight, grow to good size.

Fish wheels still turn in rivers to pick up this prize.

From Kobuk in Western Alaska comes semiprecious Jade,

from which jewelry and artifacts, by Alaska's artists are made.

Sitka Spruce — largest of them all, is Alaska's state tree

Prized by boat builders for the ocean's call.

Eight stars of gold on a field of blue

The Big Dipper and the North Star, too.

The Last Ice Age

During the last ice age - the Pleistocene Era – 2.6 million years to about 11,700 years ago when most of Northern Europe and North America were buried under massive sheets of ice, sea levels were 300 - 400 feet lower than present levels. The Scandinavian Ice Sheet extended to western Siberia covering northern portions of the British Isles, Germany, Poland and Russia. Complex icefields covered mountain in northeastern Siberia and Asia. In North America, the Laurentide Ice sheet flowed out of Northern Canada as far south as St. Louis, Missouri and extended from the east slopes of the Rocky Mountains to the Atlantic Ocean. West of the Rockies, the Cordilleran Ice sheet flowed south out of Alaska and carved out Puget Sound before grinding to a halt near present day Olympia, Washington. A land mass nearly the size of Australia was isolated north of the ice sheets; Siberia and North America were connected by a grassland mesa. Beneath the water that now separates them, the broad continental shelf is a relatively flat and featureless plain which, at its southern extreme, descends steeply to the deep Pacific basin. A thousand miles to the north, the northern edge slopes gradually into the basin of the Arctic Ocean – an ocean that possibly had a shallow ice cover, subject to seasonal changes with open water and icebergs calving from surrounding ice sheets.

In Alaska, the Tanana-Yukon River Basin was virtually ice free, with minimal glacial ice encroachment from bordering mountain ranges. Only the tips of the very tallest mountains of Alaska were visible above the vast sheets of ice covering the land. The peaks of North America's two tallest mountains, Mt. Denali – the Great One (elev. 20,310 feet) and Canada's Mt. Logan (elev. 19,551 feet) were visible. Smaller peaks (13 to 14 thousand feet) were beneath the ice and subject to shaping from glacial movement. Slowly creeping ice sculpted mountain slopes and valleys. Melting glaciers sent torrents of rushing water down mountain sides to change the slopes and valleys below even more.

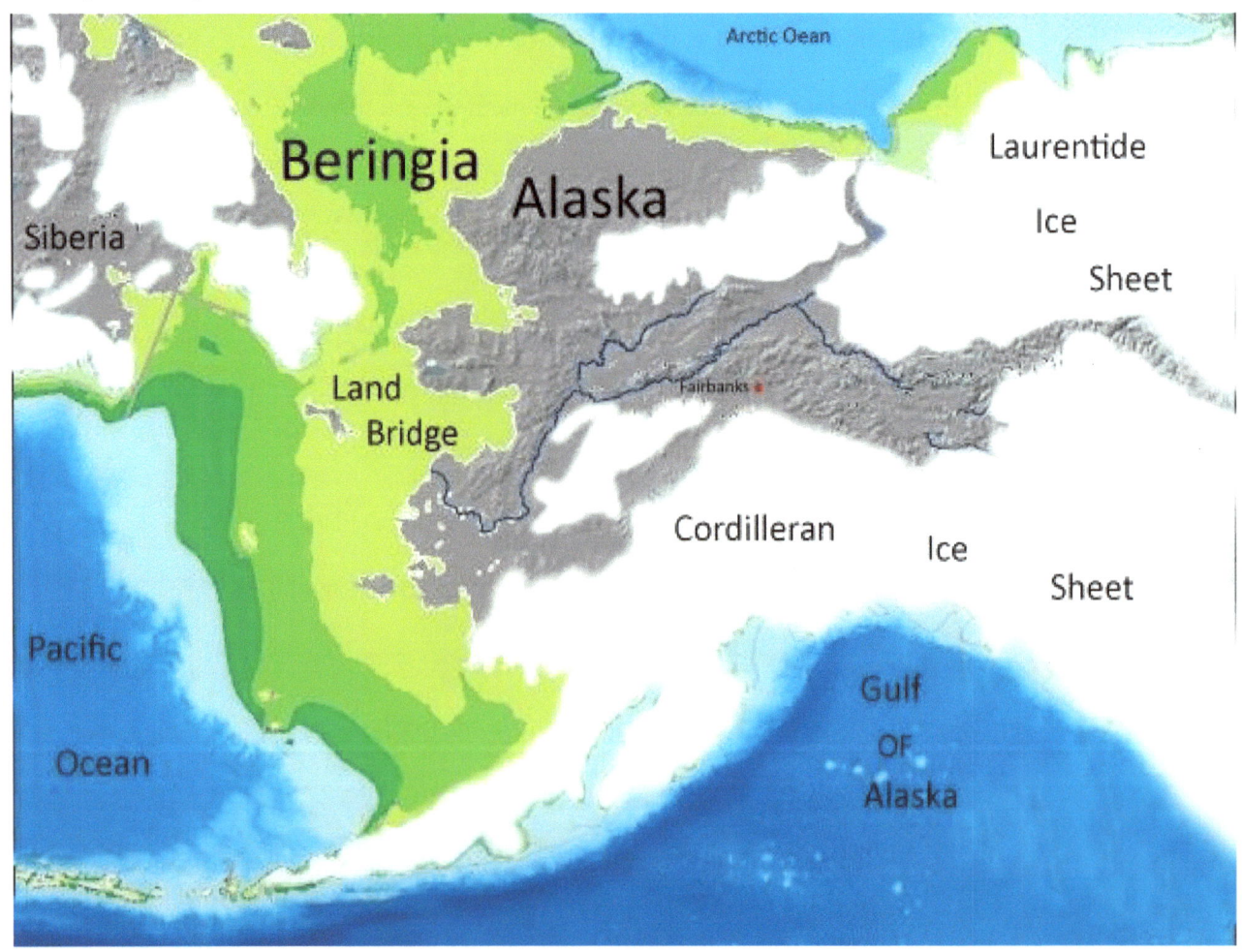

Scientists still disagree about climate and plant life and the ability of areas to support humans and large animals. What is left of Beringia would have been the higher elevations of a land as massive as Australia; the lower elevations (1,553,428 square miles) having been inundated by rising seawater. Even through the coldest times, the land bridge (Beringia) kept Pacific moisture from entering the interior areas of Alaska and north-eastern Siberia allowing the lowlands to remain ice free. Low river valleys, which formed the southeastern limits of Beringia, may have had a climate that was much colder and drier than today, and some areas may even have been as much as 50° warmer. Since a large portion of the land that helped create the climate conditions is now below the waters of the Arctic Ocean and the Bering Sea, scientists rely on fossil remains found on bordering lands. Fossil and pollen show that wildflowers and shrubs flourished and supported populations that included beetles, lemmings, ptarmigan, moose, antelope, grizzly bear, steppe bison, western camels, Pleistocene horses, and wooly rhinoceros. The first underwater survey of the sunken landforms was conducted in the Bering Sea in 1976 and since then only two more have been done. Since archeological digs on the ocean floor are not possible, scientist are limited to theories and possibilities.

Evidence suggests that, during a warm period about 30,000 years ago, before the peak of the ice age, people lived in northeast Siberia. Then, apparently, they vanished for 15,000 years. Similar tools found in Siberia and Alaska indicate that people migrated eastward across the mesa, with older samples of the tools on the Siberia side. It would have been a slow migration with an almost certain stop of nearly ten thousand years. Mutations in mitochondrial DNA found in today's Native Americans indicate a population isolated from the Siberian mainland for thousands of years - the direct ancestors of nearly all Native American tribes in North and South America – the original "first peoples". DNA links ancient North Siberians with people from the Lake Baikal region of Southern Russia, with a bit of European and East Asian and it is from the North Siberians that Native Americans derive approximately 40% of their ancestry.

As the ice receded, the land changed and, slowly, so did the climate. Over time, grasses grew on the new land and then small shrubs took root turning it into an abundant paradise. Slowly, animals extended their habitats as water advanced over the plains they had once grazed. In small groups, people followed the game they depended on to survive.

As the ice melted and the sea level rose, the land bridge was covered and Alaska became a land isolated from the rest of the world by an ocean to the west, a vast sheet of ice to the north and tall rugged ice capped mountains to the east. It remained a little known land until major world powers began seeking a northwest passage that would allow navigation from the Pacific to the Atlantic. As European explorers sailed up the west coast of the Americas, Russian sea captains took word to the Czar about a great land that lay beyond the ocean east of Siberia.

This signaled the end of Alaska's isolation and the beginning of legends that continue to hold fascination for people all over the globe. Alaska symbolizes the last frontier, the last untouched wilderness. It still retains the image of adventure and isolation. It stills holds the lure of gold, oil, unexplored resources and a better future. A fascinating history, coupled with its vast untouched wilderness, its remoteness and its stunning massive scenery acts as a magnet to draw visitors who find the land bigger and more breathtaking and awe inspiring than the legends and stories that brought them from every corner of the globe.

ALASKA

Alaska – oh what visions the name implies!

Majestic mountains and deep blue skies.

Crystal clear waters of lake and stream.

A hunter's paradise – a fisherman's dream.

A land unexplored – wild and free.

A great bald eagle on a lonely tree.

The awesome wonder of the Northern Lights

Streaking across the dark arctic nights.

Summer days when darkness doesn't fall,

Winter days when there's no light at all.

Dall sheep with rounded horn on a rocky ledge –

windswept and forlorn.

Shaggy bears – grizzly, black and brown,

Polar bears and Kodiaks – all of world renown.

Silver salmon and the giant king,

Hurrying to spawn before the geese take wing.

Oil rigs looming over barren ground

where caribou and wolves still abound.

Dog sled races over frozen snow –

daring expanses where few dare go.

The 49'ers rush for gold…

Of which stories and legends will forever be told.

There's little wonder that Alaska's name

Is touched with awe, fortune and fame.

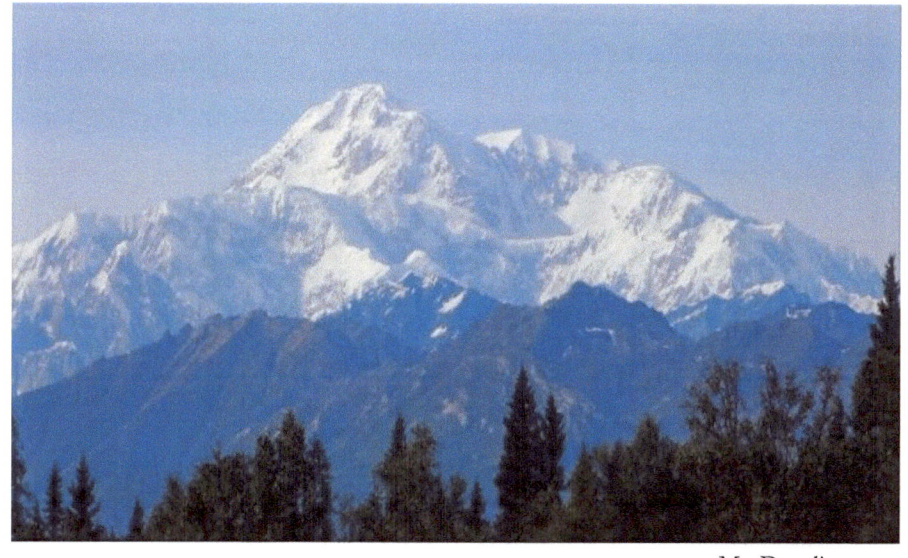

Mt. Denali

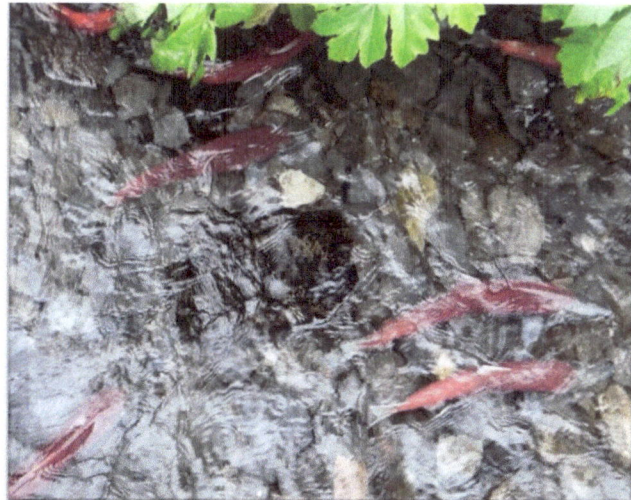

Eagle

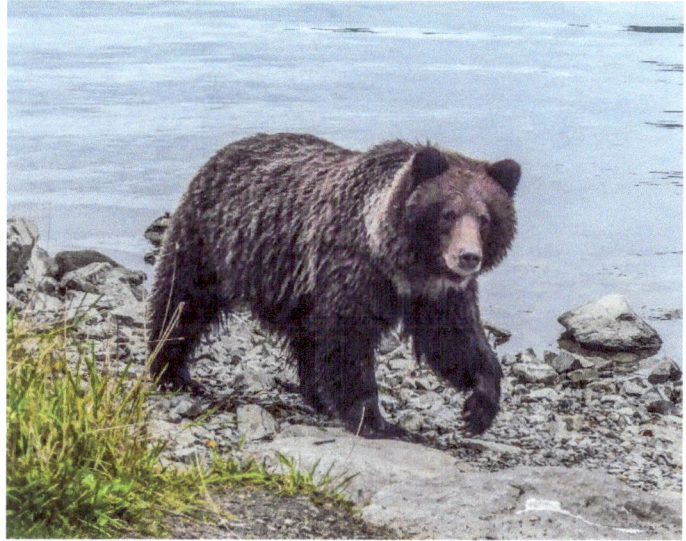

Grizzly

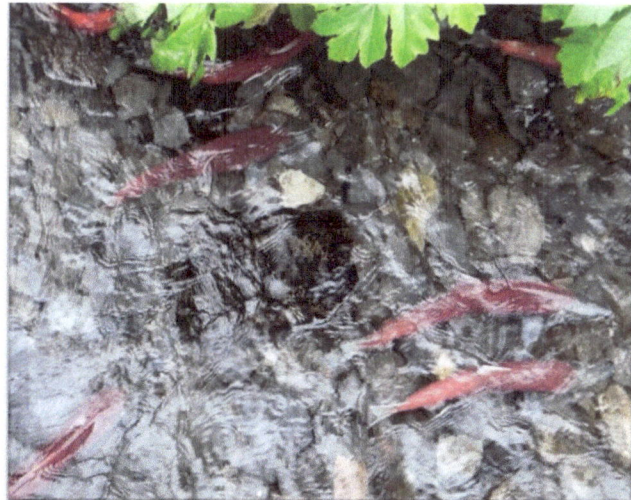

Salmon spawning

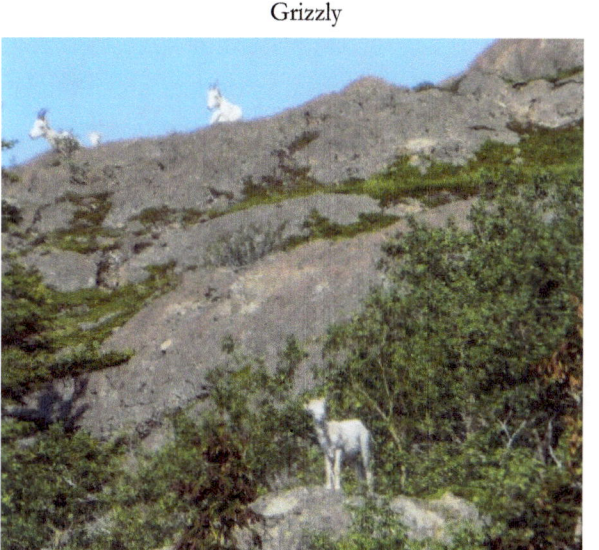

Sheep above Seward Highway - Turnagain Arm

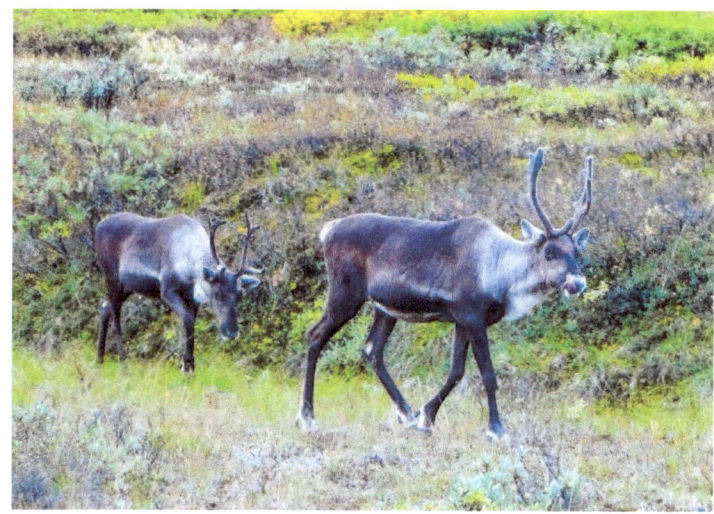

Caribou

Remnants of the Ice Age

About 23,000 years ago, a blanket of ice covered a third of the earth's surface. Isolated glaciers are all that remain of the last great ice age and they are vanishing from the face of the earth. Only 10% of the earth's surface is covered by glaciers; most of them in Arctic and Antarctic regions. Nearly all of Greenland is buried beneath glacial ice up to two miles thick in places and is so heavy that some land has been pressed below sea level. The world's largest glacier is Lambert in Antarctica. It is 270 miles long, 60 miles across at its widest point and 8,200 feet deep at the center. Lambert Glacier flows up to 2,600 feet a year.

In the continental Unite States, less than 200 sq. miles of glacial ice remain and most of these are found in nine western states – in the Rocky Mountains or further west. Washington's Mt. Rainier (14,410 ft.) is the most glaciated mountain in the Lower 48 states; Mt. Baker, (10,778 ft.) north of Seattle, is the second. Lilliput Glacier on Mt. Stewart (12,291 ft.) in Sequoia National Park in California's Central Valley is the southern most glacier in the U.S.

An estimated 100,000 glaciers cover 5% of Alaska and fewer than 700 have been officially named. The two largest - Malaspina and Bering – each larger than Rhode Island - cover more than 2,000 sq. miles. The base of Malaspina may be 1,000 ft. below sea level from where it towers to a thickness of about 2,000 ft.

Bagley Icefield in Southeastern Alaska, is the largest nonpolar icefield in North America. As thick as 3,000 feet in some areas, it is 127 miles long and extends over 1,900 sq. miles of Alaska, British Columbia and the Yukon. It covers most of the central core of the St. Elias Mountains and part of the Chugach.

Bering Glacier, North America's largest and longest glacier, flows out of the icefield and the Wrangell-St. Elias Mountains terminating in Vitus Lake, about 10 miles from the Gulf of Alaska. The glacier and its lake provide some of the most spectacular glacier and alpine scenery in the world with the lake holding a jumble of giant icebergs up to 1,500 feet long. Despite the fact that it is, like the icefield it is part of, slowly receding, it surges forward about every 20 years or so – the last surge, a small one, occurred in 2008-2009. Bering is the largest temperate surging glacier on earth. Since 1989, it has been a leading research site for the study of glacial surging, drastic retreat and the dynamics of iceberg calving. Its location in the Wrangell-St. Elias Range places it over the boundary between two tectonic plates – the Pacific Plate and the North American Plate. The weight of Bering kept the boundary stabilized, but as it loses mass, diminished pressure allows rocks along the fault line to move more freely, resulting in more earthquakes.

Harding Icefield, which covers 700 square miles on Alaska's Kenai Peninsula, is one of four major ice caps in the Unite States. This remnant of a massive Pleistocene ice sheet that once covered over half of Alaska now stretches more than 50 miles from the Resurrection River to the divide in the Kenai Mountains. Rising 6,612 feet above sea level, Tuuli Peak, the highest point in the Kenai Mountains peeks out of the ice, an indication that the icefield may be a mile deep in some places. Exit Glacier, near Seward, is one of over 30 glaciers flowing out of this field; eight are tidewater glaciers that calve icebergs into scenic fjords along the gulf of Alaska.

North America's fifth largest icefield, the Juneau Icefield (100 miles long and 45 miles wide) covers over 1,500 sq. miles stretching north of Juneau and across the border into British Columbia. It feeds more than 40 large valley glaciers and 100 smaller ones. One of its best known glaciers is Mendenhall, a major tour attraction on the outskirts of Juneau. Taku, the largest outlet glacier of the Juneau Icefield is a tidewater glacier. At 1,477 miles thick, the 36 mile long glacier is the deepest and thickest alpine temperate glacier in the world. On the west side of the icefield, an icefall formed where Vaughn Lewis Glacier joins the larger Gilkey Glacier, creating distinct flowing waves of ice. Llewellyn Glacier, the second largest glacier in the Juneau Icefield, is a large valley glacier in the St. Elias Mountains near Haines Junction, Yukon Territory. It has advanced and retreated many times and blocked the Alsek River creating a lake that once occupied the valley where Haines Junction is located as late as the mid to late 1800s. Evidence indicates the lake was 60 miles long and 650 ft. deep. When the glacial dam failed, a catastrophic flood followed. The lake may have emptied in three days at the current rate of flow of the Amazon River – 60 million gallons per second.

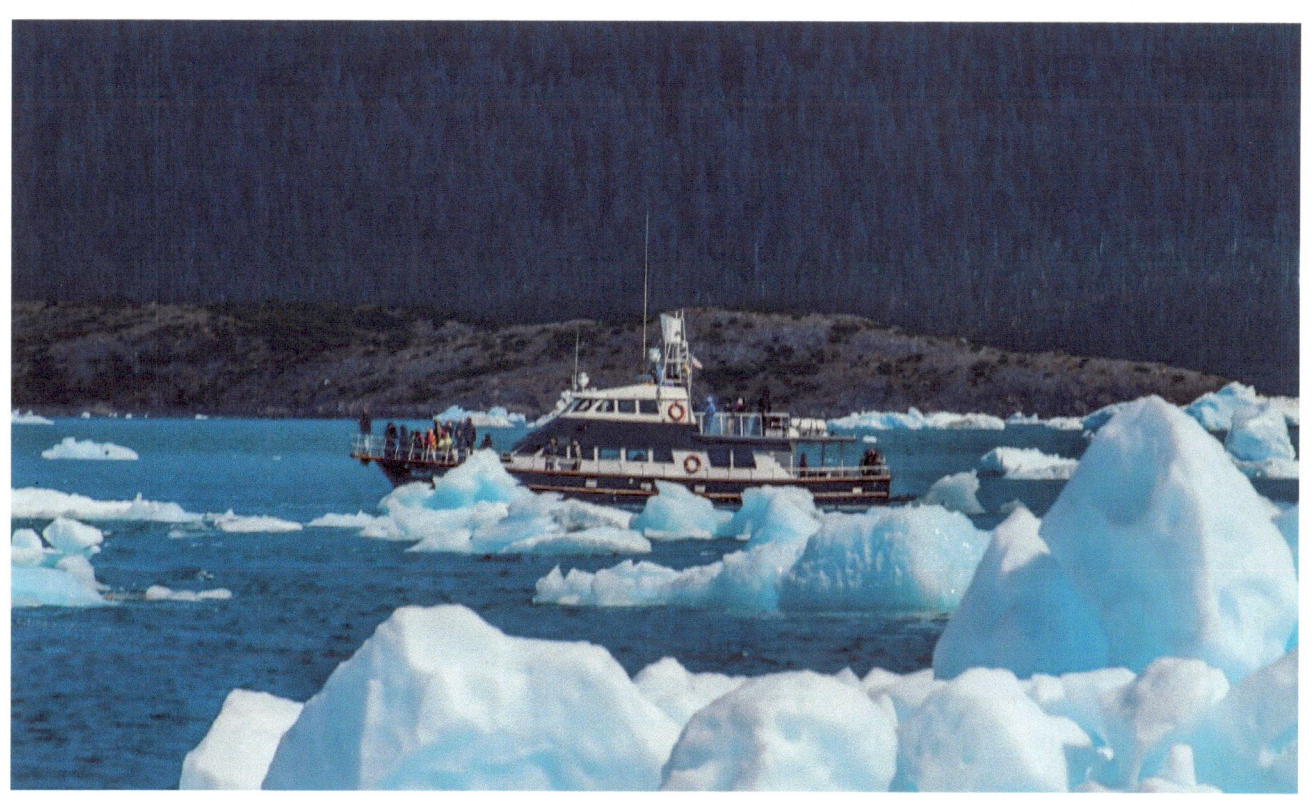

Columbia Glacier

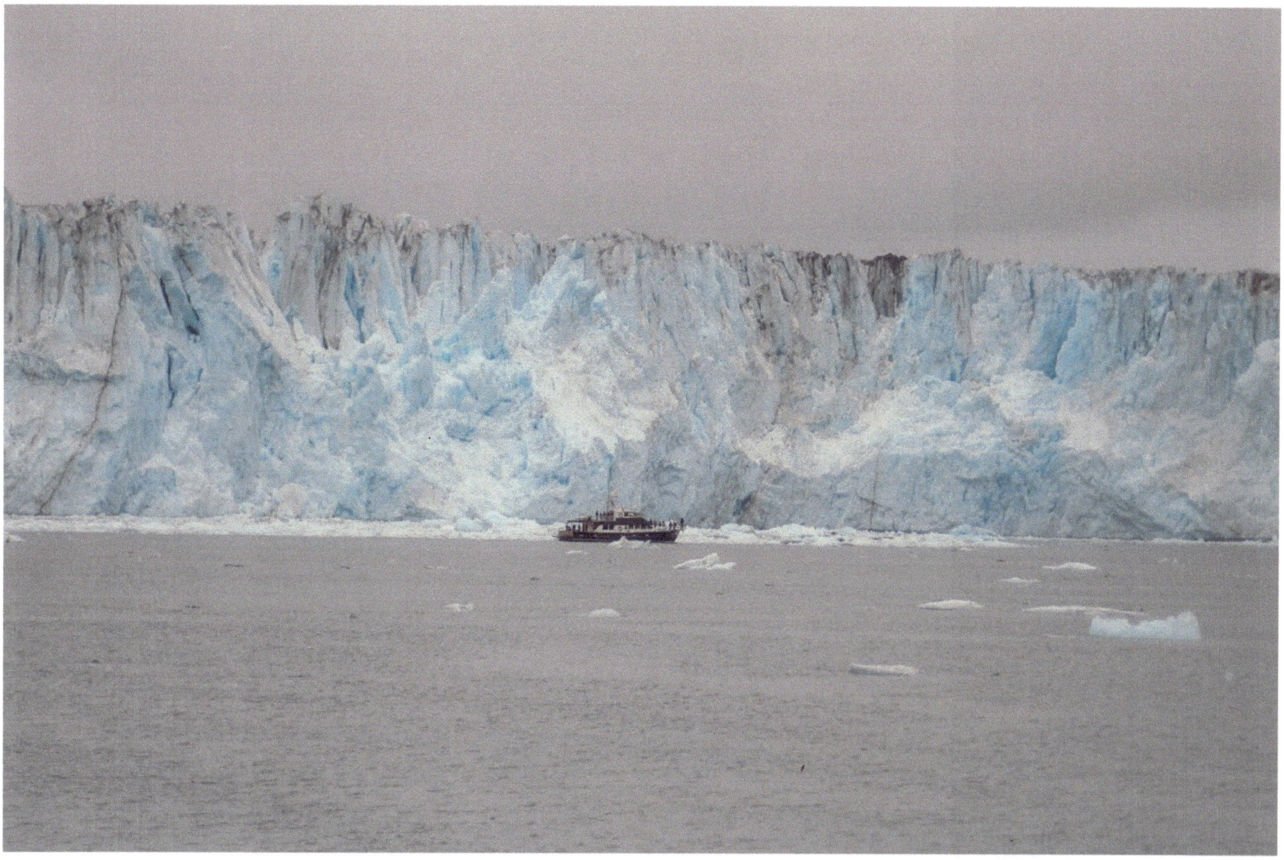

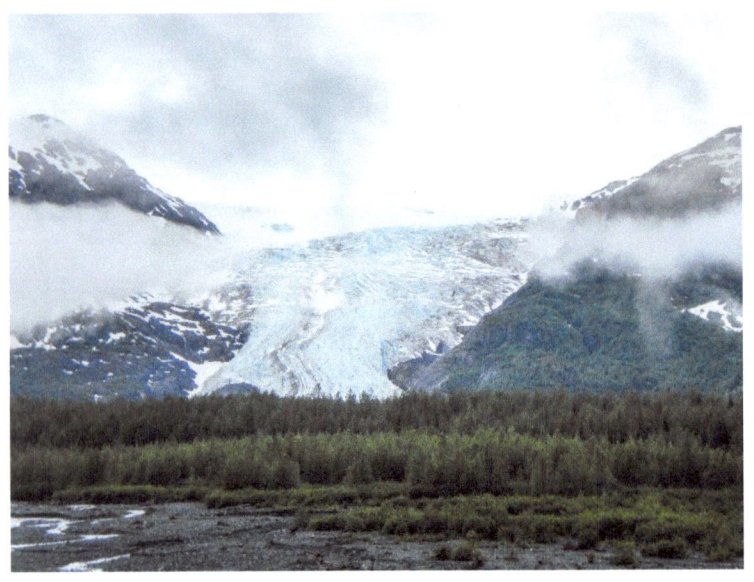

Exit Glacier near Seward

Exit Glacier, 3.7 miles from Seward (12 road miles), is one of 38 glaciers flowing out of the Kenai Mountain's Harding Icefield. It began its journey during the Little Ice Age (1350 – 1870) and by 1815 had advanced to within 1.25 miles of the Resurrection River. Signs along the road to the ranger station and the path up to the glacier's face delineate the glacier's slow retreat from its terminal moraine in 1815 to its present location. In the spring of 1968, a party of ten completed the first ever recorded successful crossing of Harding Icefield. They exited the icefield on Resurrection Glacier, but because it was referred to as the 'exit glacier', newspaper reports named it 'Exit Glacier'.

The largest vehicle accessible glacier in the state is a river of ice that flows from high up in the Northern Chugach Mountains and terminates in the valley below. The four mile wide face of the Matanuska Glacier lies 26 miles from its source. Although the Matanuska is receding, it advanced several times during the twentieth century. For 60 days in the summer in 1979, it surged forward more than 100 feet. As it recedes from the valley it once filled, it leaves behind a moraine – tons of silt, rocks and boulders it pushed before it for thousands of years.

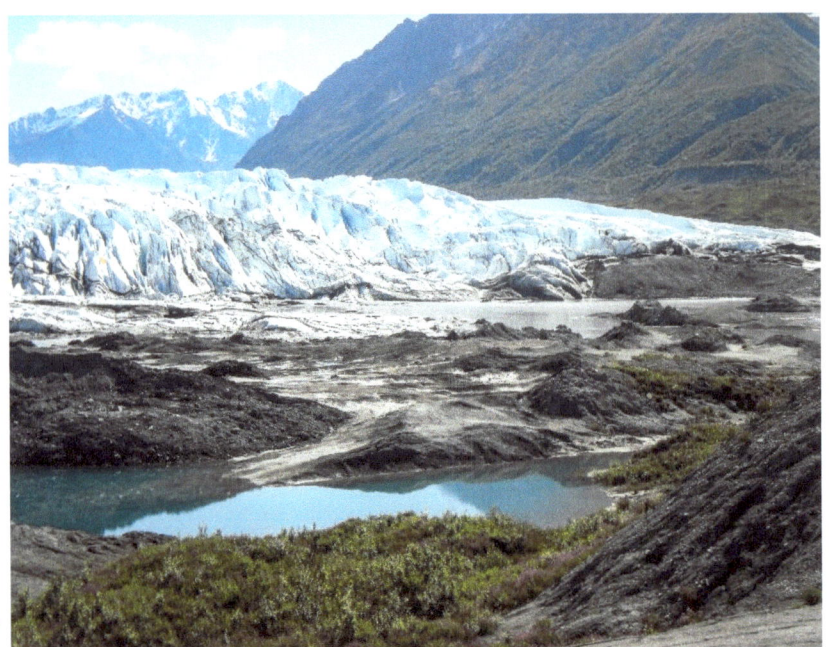

Matanuska Glacier near Palmer

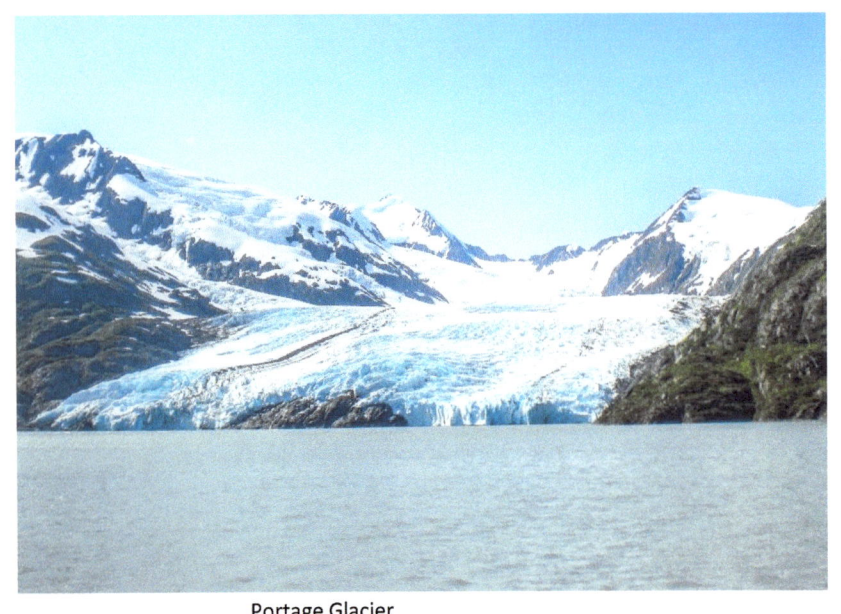

Portage Glacier

Massive ice sheets once covered the 4,000 ft. peaks towering above Portage Pass in the Chugach Range. Explorer, Burns, Middle, Byron, and Shakespeare glaciers - still massive glaciers on their own - are remnants of these giants. The best known glacier, however, is Portage. Now six miles long, it once filled the length of the 14 mile long valley it carved out. In 1914, a lake began to form at the face of the rapidly receding glacier. The now three mile long lake is 700 feet deep at the face of the glacier and is often dotted by bergs calving off the glacier.

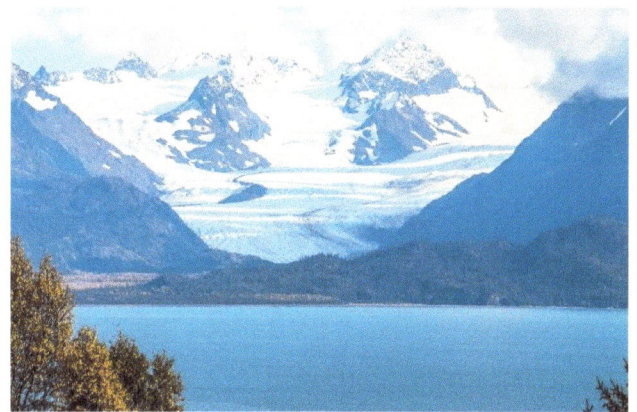
Dixon and Portlock Glaciers near Homer

Dixon and Portlock Glaciers (6 miles long) are both mountain glaciers that overlook Homer across Kachemak Bay. They are part of the Grewingk-Yalik Icefield which encompasses approximately 30 sq. miles south of the Harding Icefield.

Harding Icefield's Bear Glacier (13 miles long), is the longest glacier in Kenai Fiords National Park. It calves into a 300 – 500 ft. deep, 3.5 sq. mile fresh water lake.

Aialik, the largest of Harding Icefield's glaciers, flows four miles from its source at 5,847 ft. The face, 200 ft. high, calves into Aialik Bay.

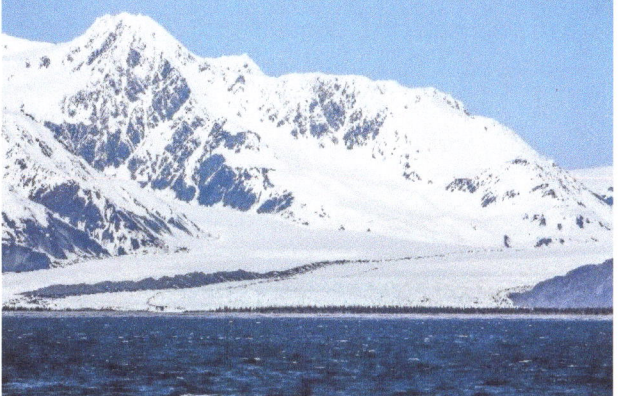
Bear Glacier near Seward

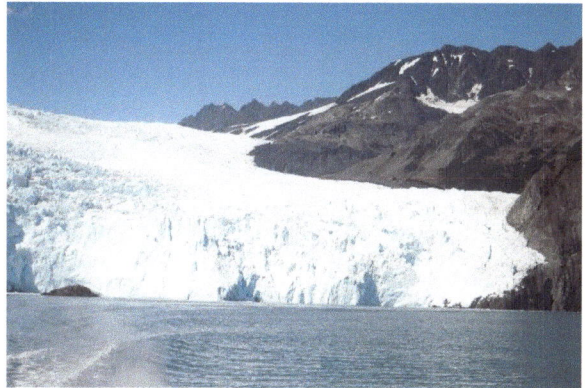
Aialik Glacier

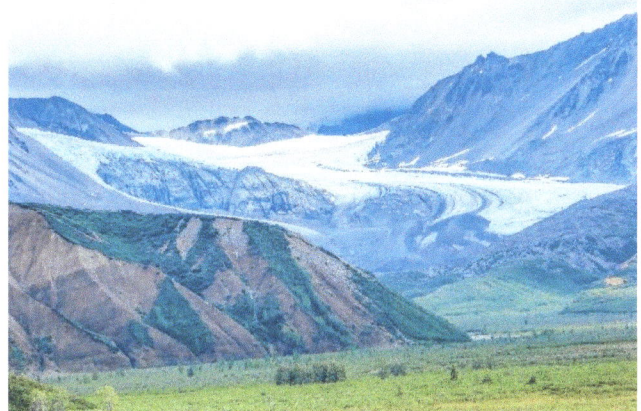
Gulkana Glacier – East of the Richardson Highway

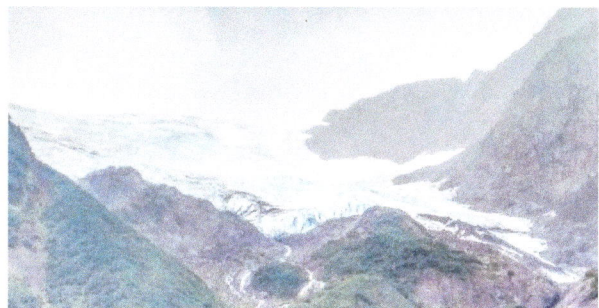
Explorer Glacier – Portage Valley

3,241 foot Isabel Pass in the Alaska Range lies roughly halfway between Fairbanks and Valdez on the Richardson Highway. Higher up, at 6,000 feet, lies the birthplace of Gulkana Glacier. The two-mile long glacier, with its two channels, is visible four miles from the road. The east arm is approximately 750 feet thick and the western about 400 feet.

Glaciers have played a hand in sculpting the features of our land. Slow moving rivers of ice - snow that fell thousands of years ago - are all that remain of the massive ice sheets that once covered most of Europe and North America. ¾ of the earth's fresh water is locked up in this ancient glacial ice.

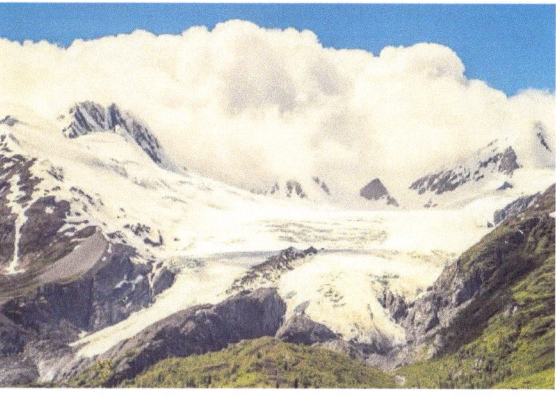
Worthington Glacier on Thompson Pass near Valdez

Worthington, on Thompson Pass 20 miles north of Valdez, is Alaska's most accessible glacier. Average snowfall on the pass is about 550 inches a year and new snow continues to add to its depth.

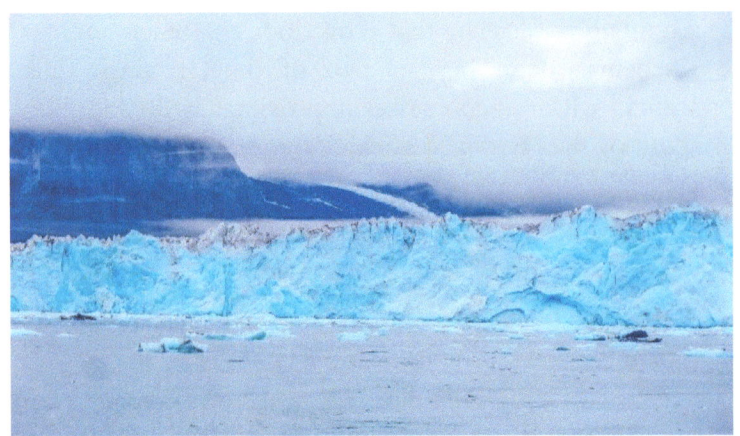

Columbia Glacier – above and below

The greatest concentration of Alaska's glaciers is in Prince William Sound. From 10,000 feet above sea level, ice flows down into separate fiords ending in individual glaciers. There are several glaciers in 25 mile long College Fiord - all named after prestigious centers of learning. Columbia Glacier, one of the world's fastest changing glaciers, is 35 miles long and covers more than 430 square miles. The retreating glacier has thinned dramatically losing about half of its thickness and volume causing one of its branches to reverse its flow direction creating two separate glaciers. Columbia Glacier accounts for nearly half of the ice loss in the Chugach Mountains.

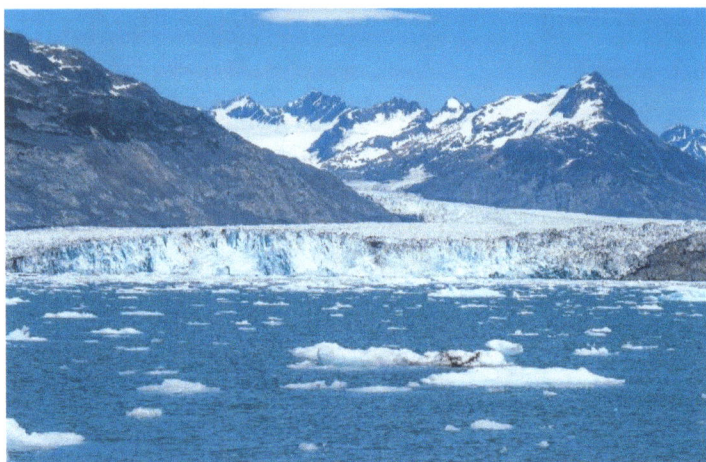

Tracy Arm, 45 miles south of Juneau, extends about 25 miles into a breathtaking canyon where sheer walls of solid granite climb from water level to 2,000 feet. Behind them tower snow capped mountain peaks as high as 7,000 feet. Thin streams of water tumble down the sheer walls in cascading falls. This spectacular waterway ends at the foot of twin glaciers – Sawyer and South Sawyer.

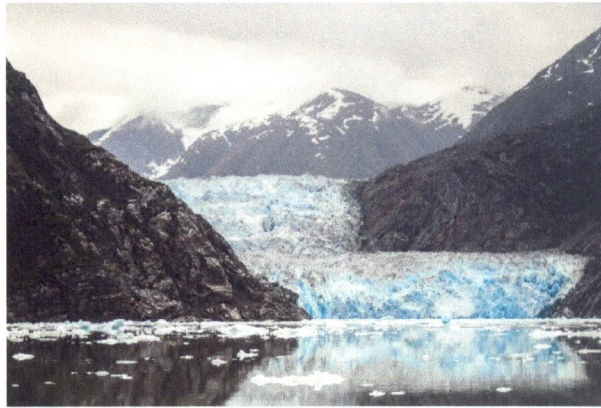

Sawyer Glacier near Juneau

South Sawyer Glacier is separated from Sawyer Glacier by a mountain. Both of these glaciers are part of the Stikine Icefield on the crest of the Cost Mountains spanning the U.S./Canadian border near Juneau. Approximately 20 miles long, it covers more than 100 square miles.

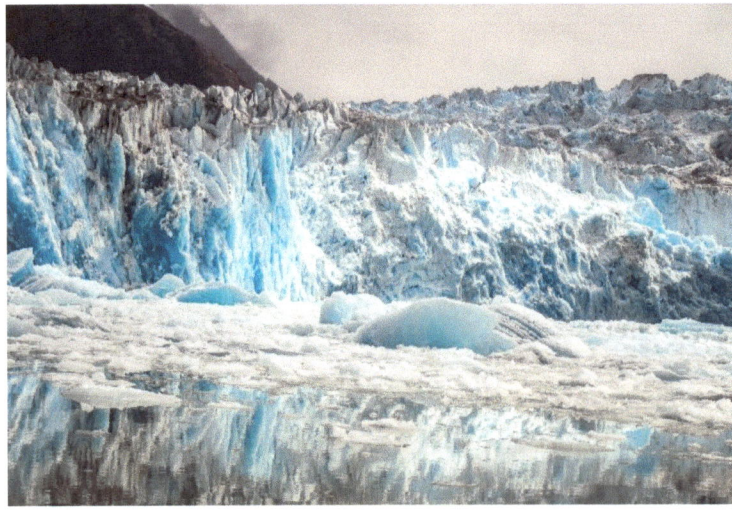

South Sawyer Glacier

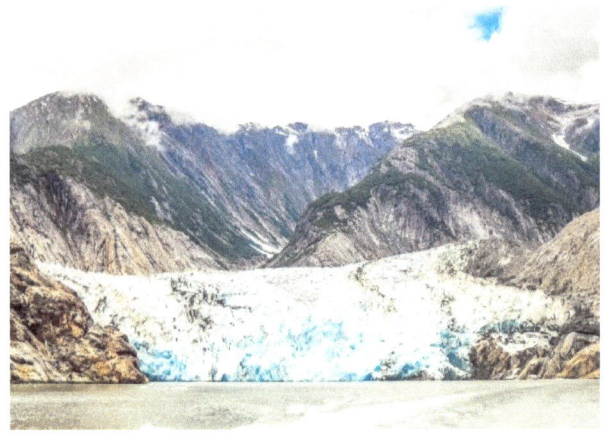

Sawyer Glacier

CALVING AT AIALIK GLACIER

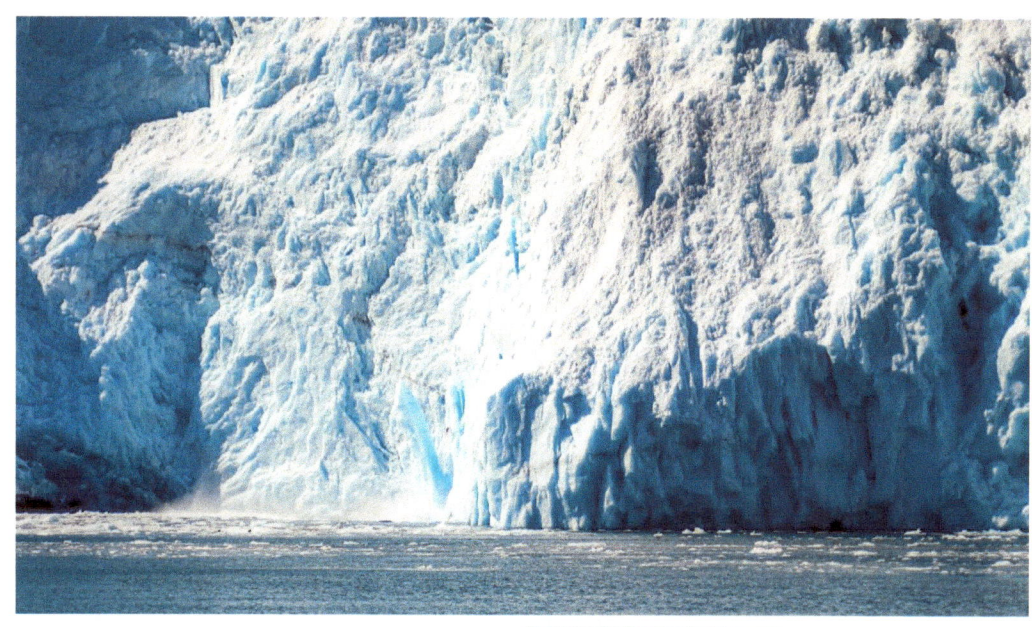

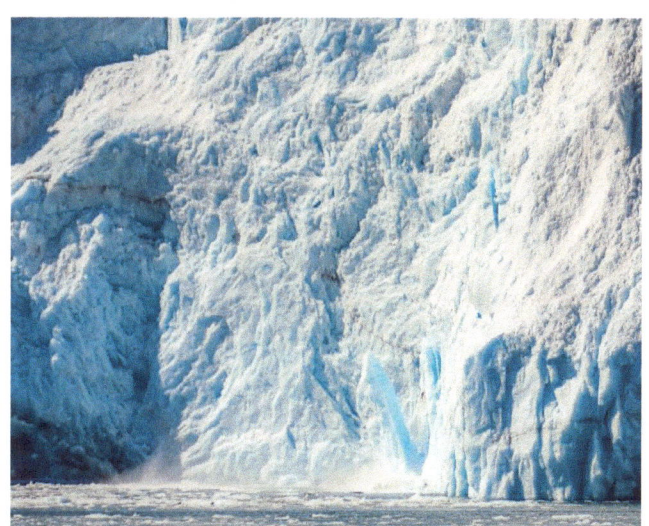

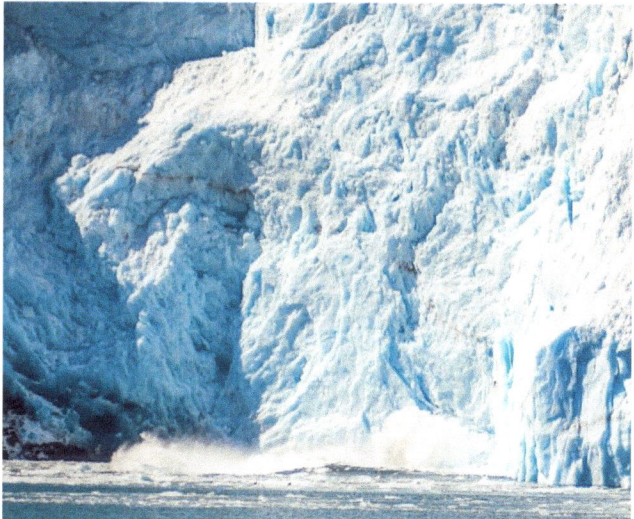

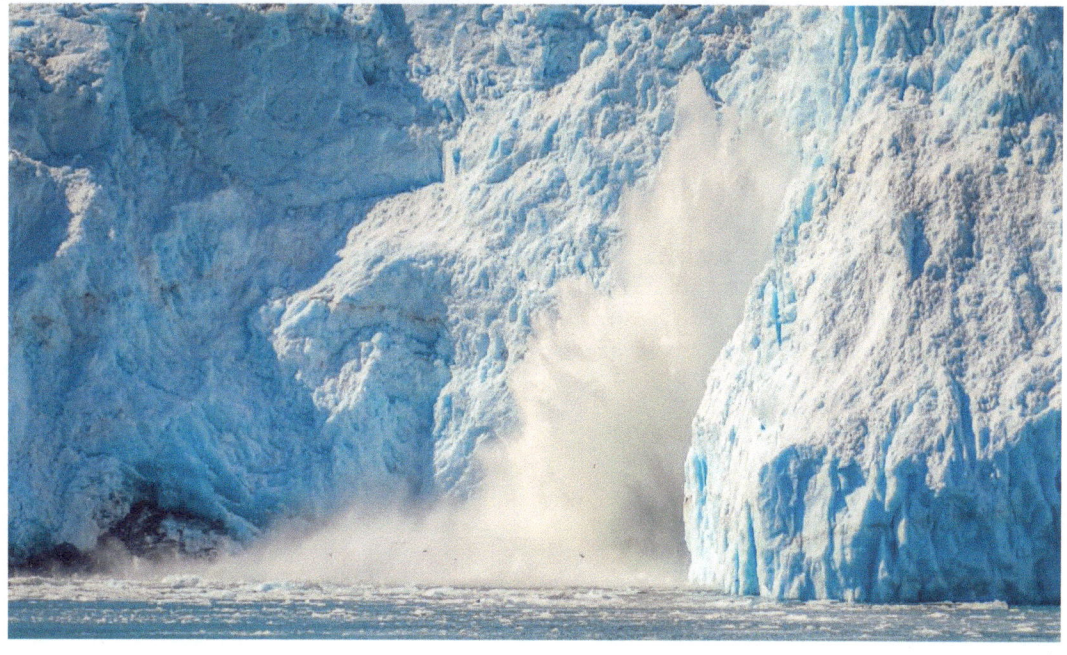

PATTERNS IN THE ICE
Portage Lake

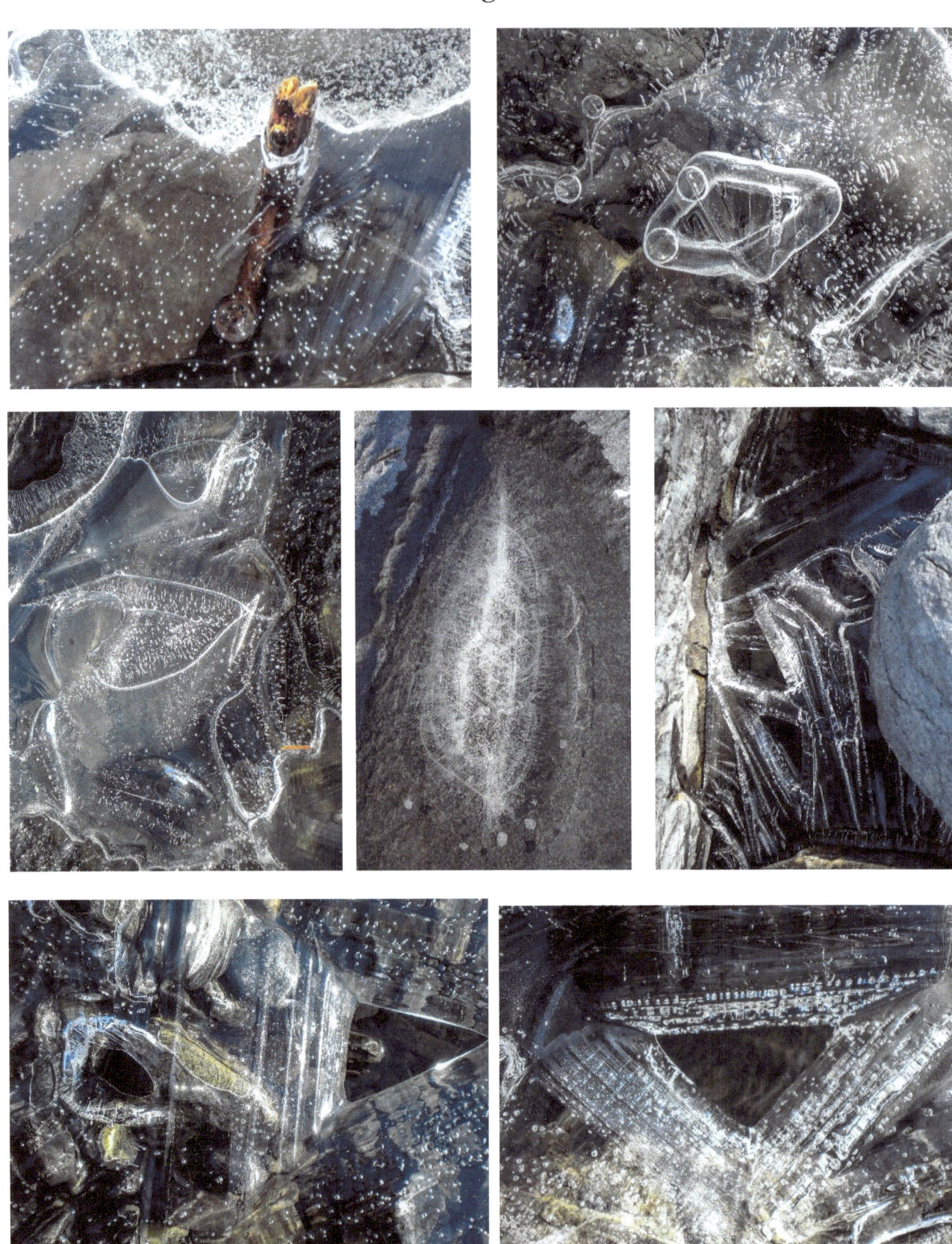

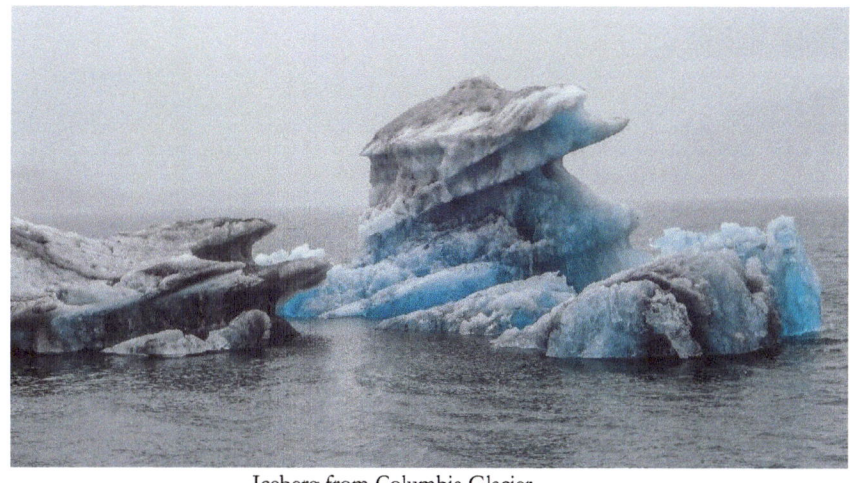
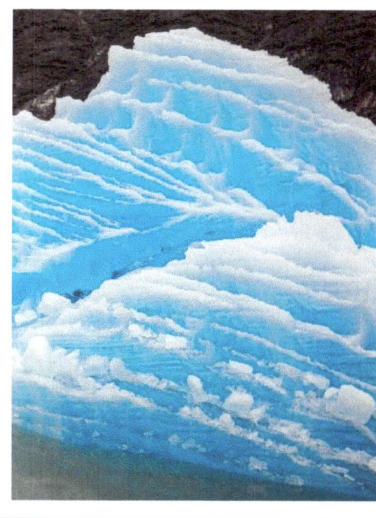

Iceberg from Columbia Glacier

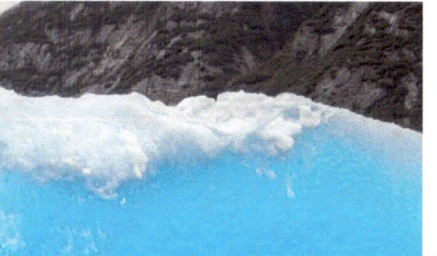
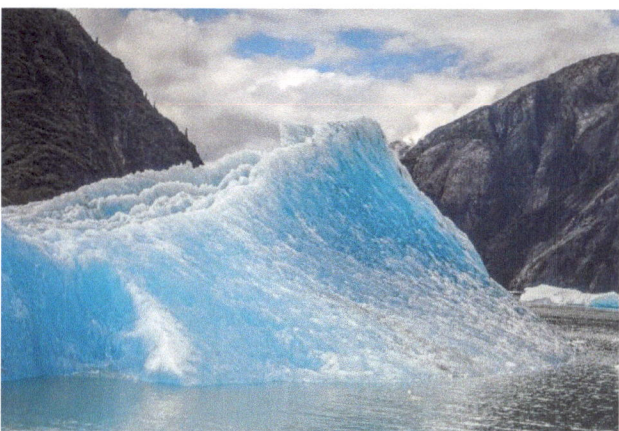

Icebergs from South Sawyer Glacier

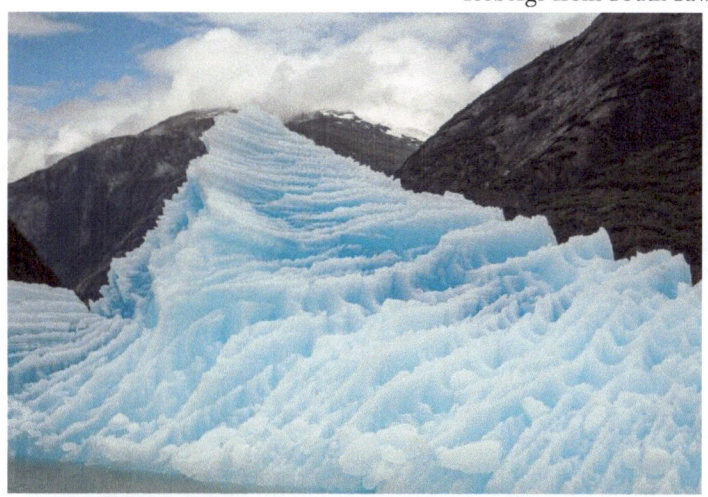
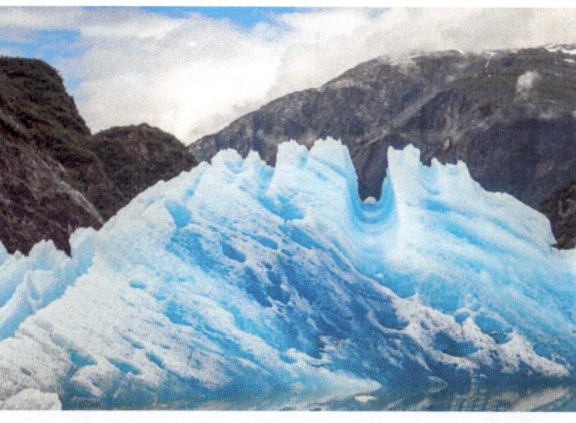
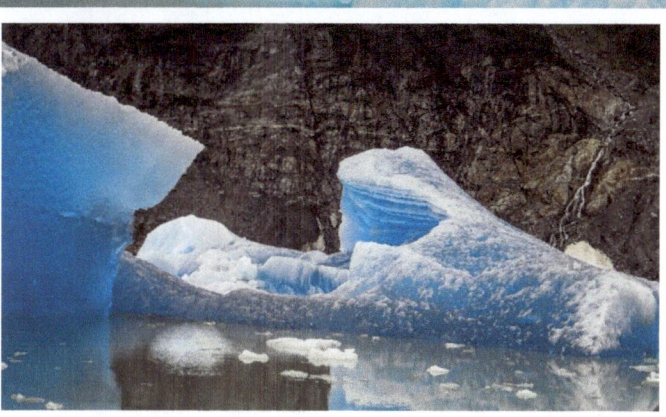
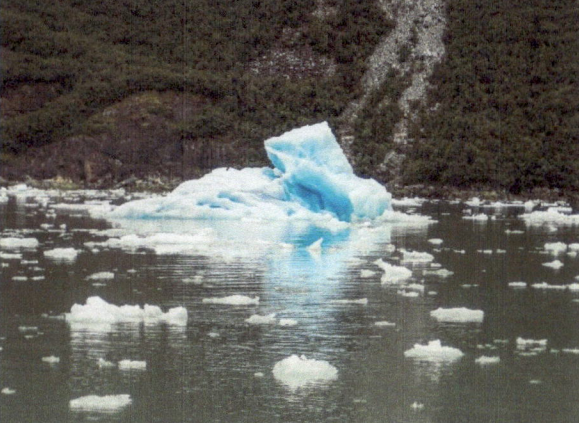

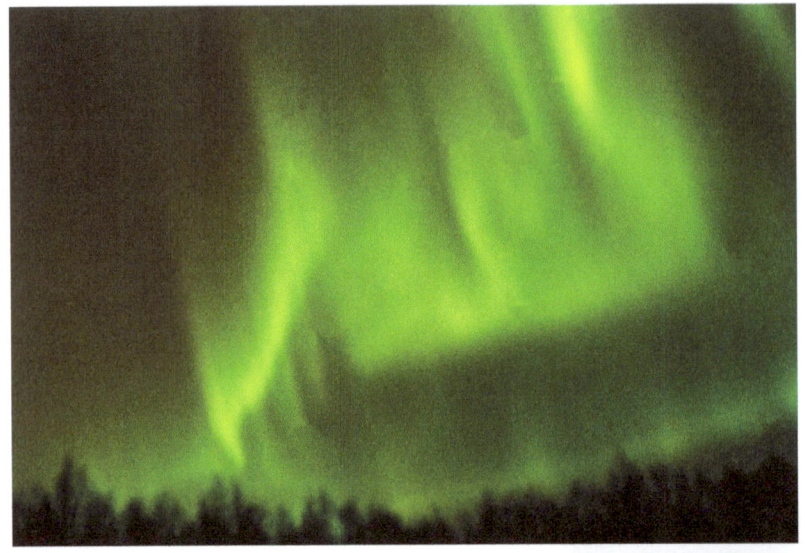

The sun is a constantly exploding ball of gases; gases which contain traces of the sun's magnetic field. Those gases are sent out into space as the solar wind. The magnetosphere surrounding the earth prevents most of these particles from entering our atmosphere.

When the solar wind encounters earth, it flows around it much as water flows around a rock in a stream.

The gases that do enter the upper atmosphere begin interacting with the earth's gases creating color in the same manner as color is created in neon bulbs.

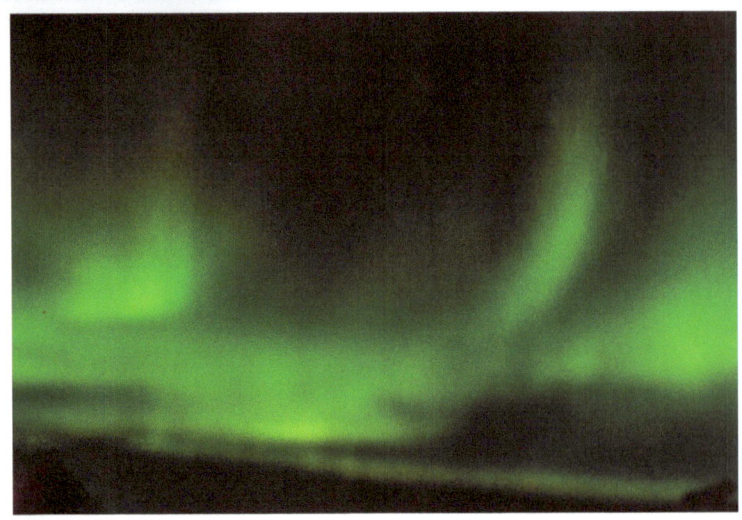

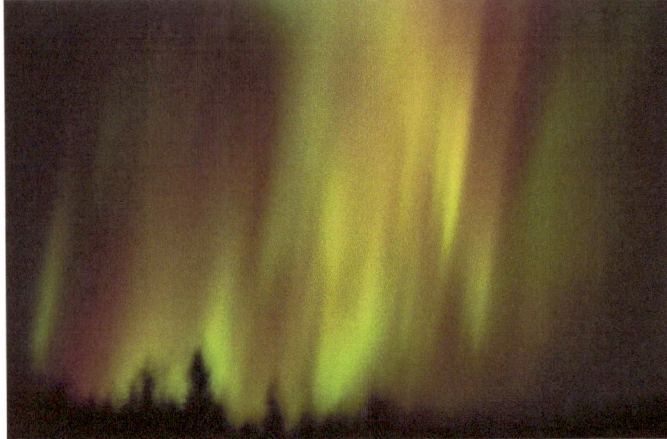

Different gases produce different colors. Oxygen over 200 miles above the earth glows red. At 60 miles, it glows yellow green. Ionic nitrogen glows blue, neutral nitrogen glows red-purple with rippled edges.

Movement of the lights is created by attraction and repulsion between particles charged by the magnetic fields of both the sun and the earth. The Southern Aurora, also known as the Aurora Australis, is an exact mirror image of the Northern Lights or the Aurora Borealis.

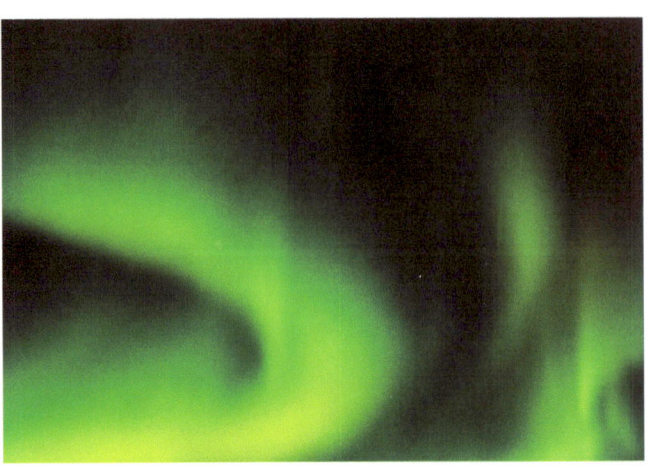

THE LIGHTS OF HEAVEN

Words are inept tools
in the mouths of men and fools
who even begin to try
to describe the events
in the dark arctic sky.

Who is the artist who mixes the paint
and swirls it softly ever so faint?
Who enables the power
to create such a cascading shower?

How many men since the dawn of time
have tried to set the words to rhyme?
To explain the powerful awesome sight;
the scenes of heavenly glory
arcing through the night?

Every language known to mankind
is unable to find
the means by which to tell
of the mesmerizing spell.

There is no justice in the pen or brush
which vainly attempts
to portray the rush
of brilliant pulsing folds of light
undulating and curling
with awe inspiring might.

One must stand in the frigid cold
to experience and behold
the awesome splendor
of the Northern Lights
from horizon to horizon
on most winter nights.

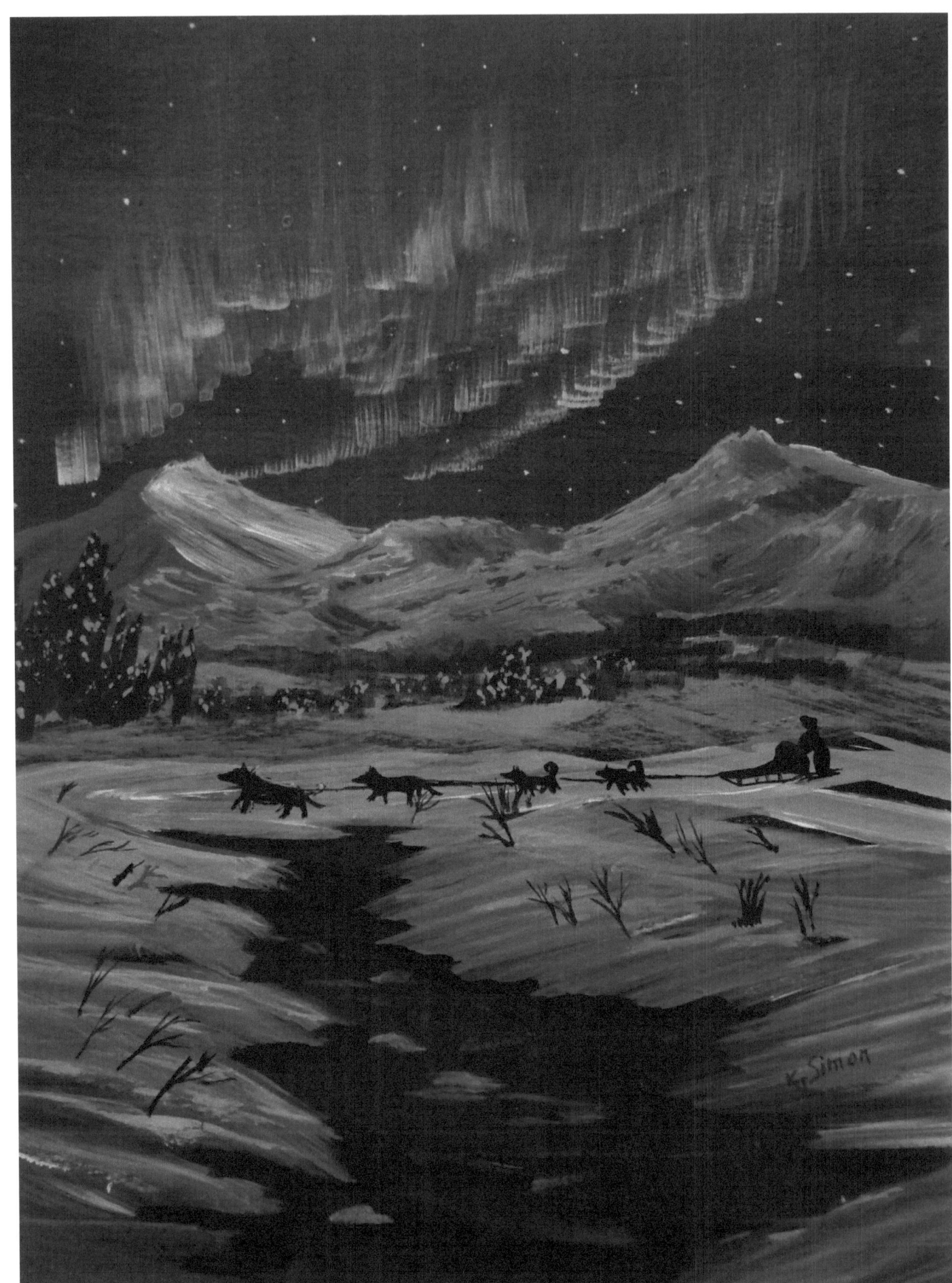

NORTHERN LIGHTS OVER ALASKA

The arctic night is long and still
When o'er the dark and distant hill
A faint touch in the ebony sky,
A glimmer of light seen on high.

Faint it appears in the dark of the night.
Stronger it grows and spreads its light
In bands that waver and gracefully flow,
It arcs the sky, moving fast, then slow.

Veils of color, transparent and clear
Grow in intensity as they draw ever near,
Pulsing and swaying in spirals and bands,
Weaving continual glistening, gossamer strands.

An enchanting, mystical spellbinding scene
Leaving one peaceful, awed and serene.
A heavenly drama, performed it seems,
Nowhere on earth...except in our dreams.

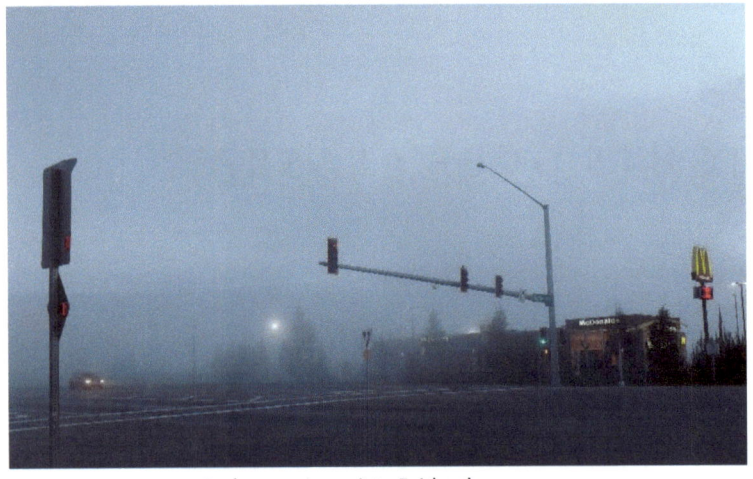

Early morning mist - Fairbanks

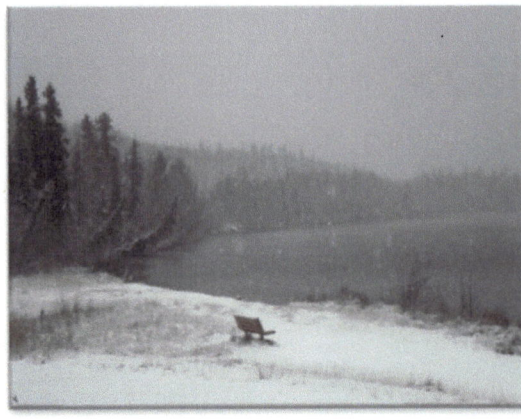

Mist over Birch Lake

Off Farmers Loop Rd.

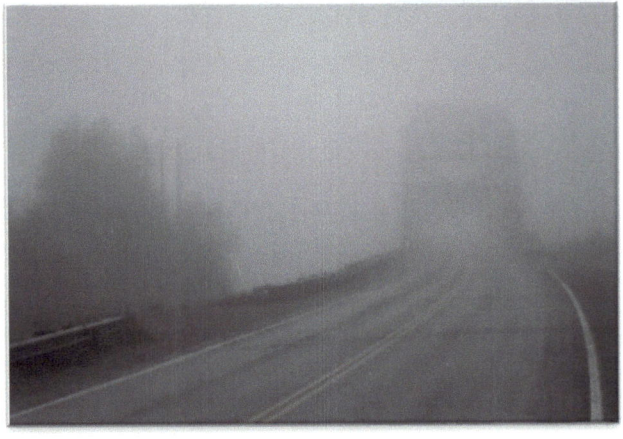

Tanana River bridge near Delta

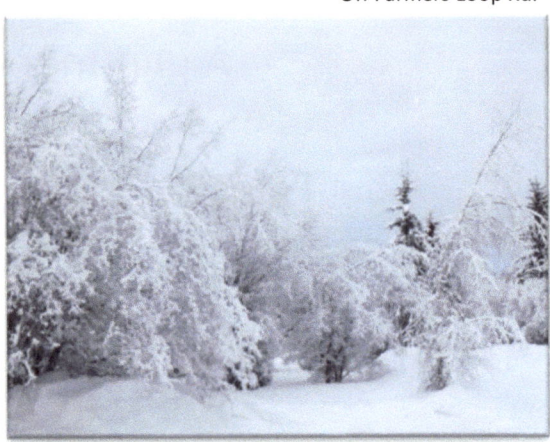

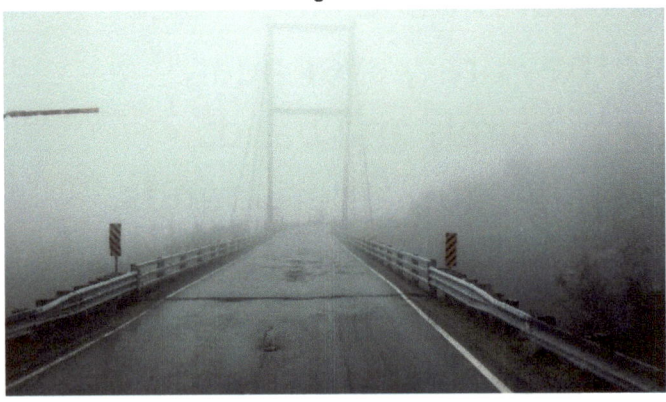

Moore Creek Bridge north of Skagway

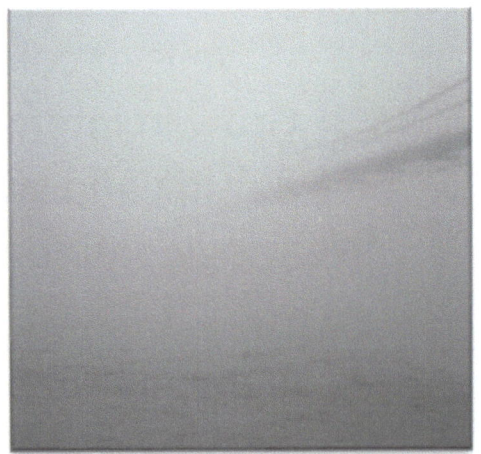

TransAlaska Pipeline crossing Tanana River at Delta

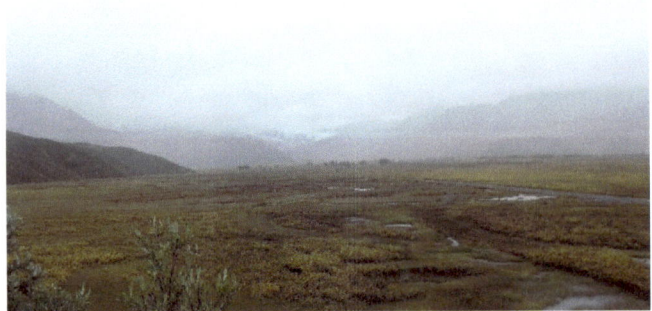

North of Valdez.

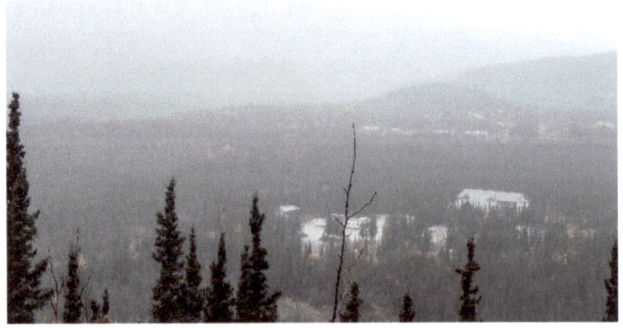

Overlooking Denali Park buildings

ICE FOG

Its wintertime and Fairbanks is covered with snow.

The mercury dropped – its 20 below.

Fences and trees are lined in frost.

Its a magical world where one can get lost.

Tendrils of mist rise from the ground;

from the rivers and slough and ponds all around.

With a life all its own, it rises on high

Wreathing and spreading til it blocks out the sky.

Exhaust and smoke are mingled within

While slowly it falls,

enfolding the city and all of its din.

The ice fog moves and, as it swirls,

it creates an eerie, ghostly world.

Headlight beams faint within its spell.

Only fog and strobe lights penetrate it well.

Structures and people are shadows

all dimly seen through the misty wall.

Seen from above or the height of a hill,

the entire valley it seems to fill

With a primeval sea – silent and still –

with hills and valleys rising out of its midst

Eerily outlined against the swirling peaks of the mist.

The sky above can be clear and blue,

but none of the light will ever get through.

The moon and the stars are hidden from sight,

While even the darkness is misty at night.

WINTER WONDERLAND

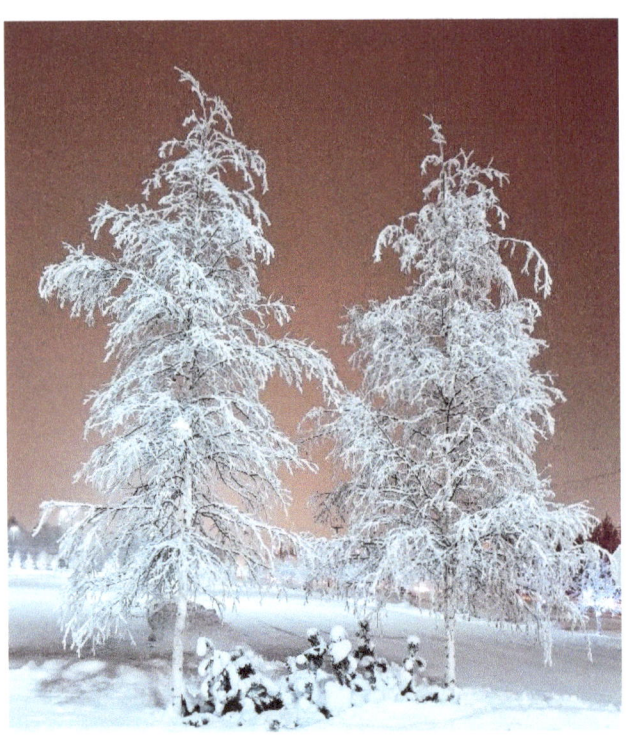

Pioneer Park – river mist and Christmas lights

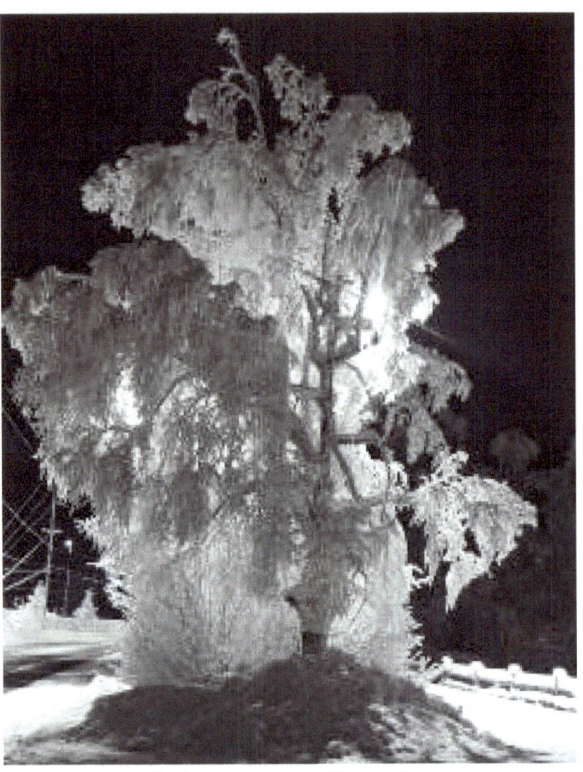

Frost laden tree near Chena River

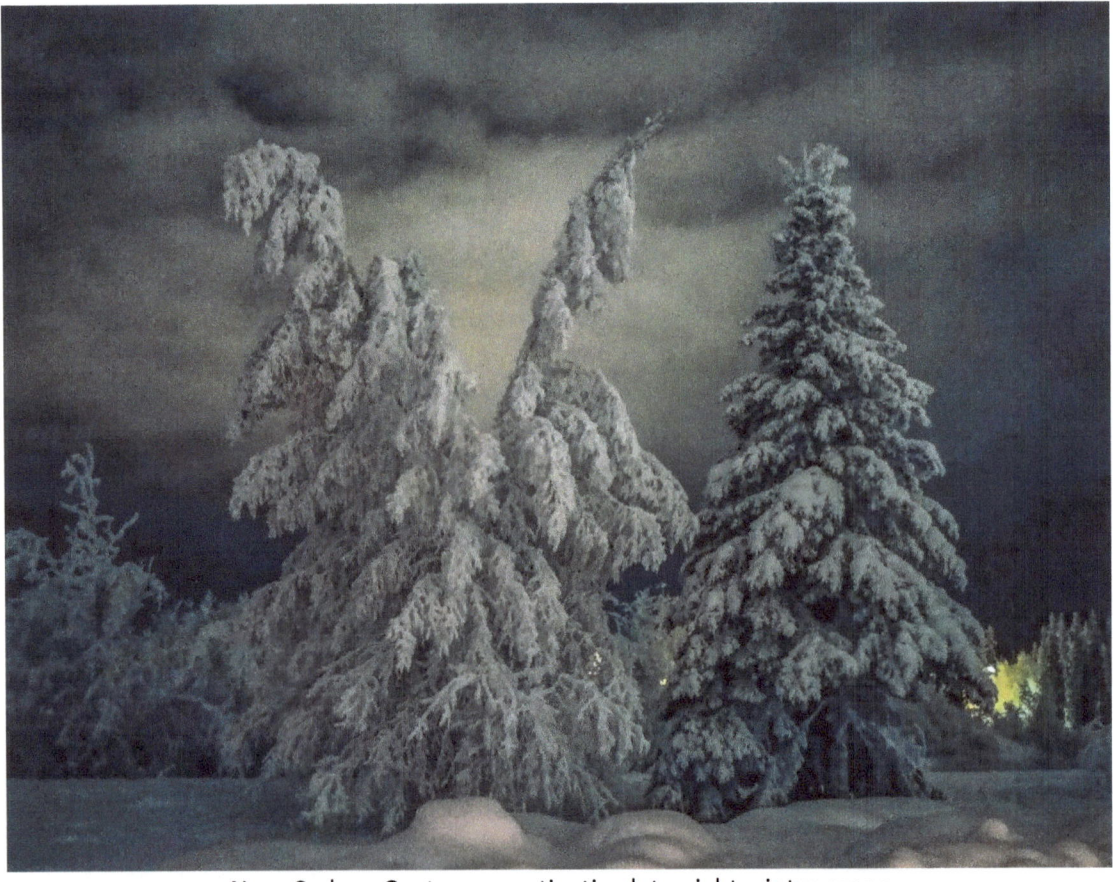

Near Carlson Center , a captivating late night winter scene

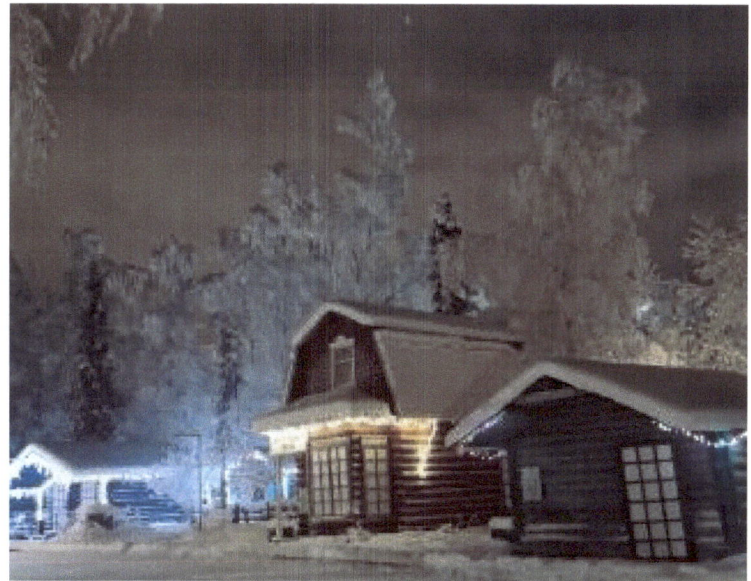

Kitty Hensley House (red) in Pioneer Park

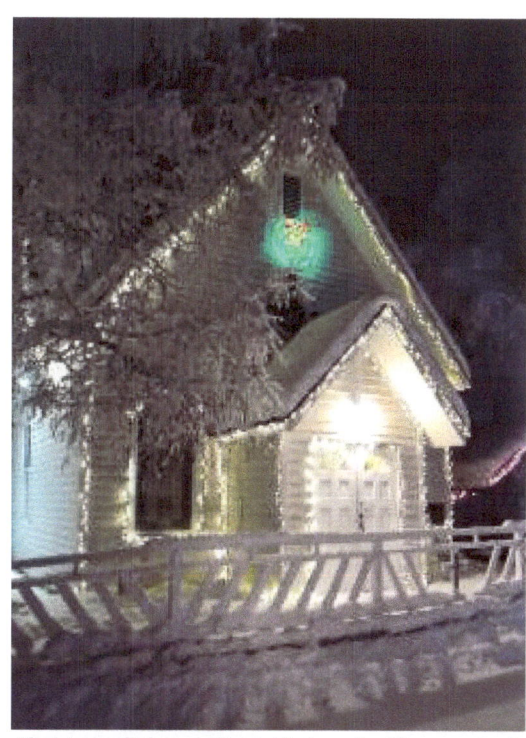

Christmas lights on the old church - Pioneer Park

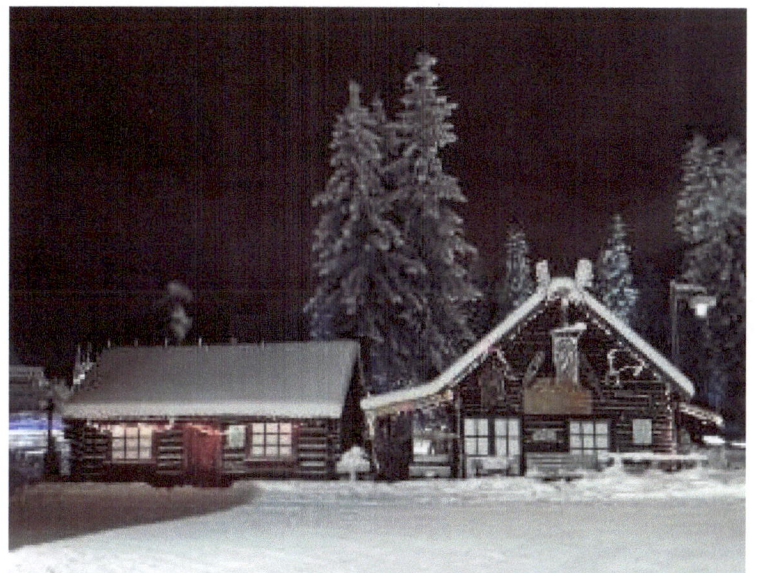

Old buildings from downtown Fairbanks - Pioneer Park

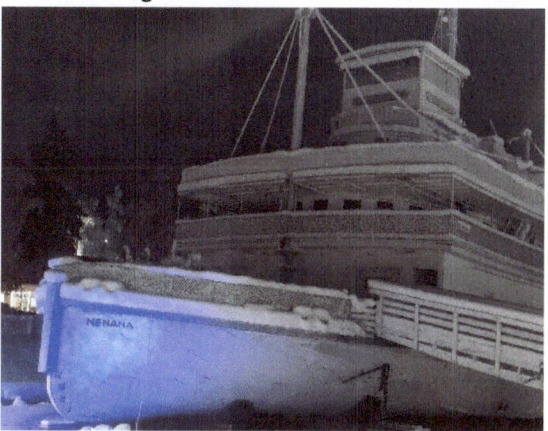

S.S. Nenana - Pioneer Park

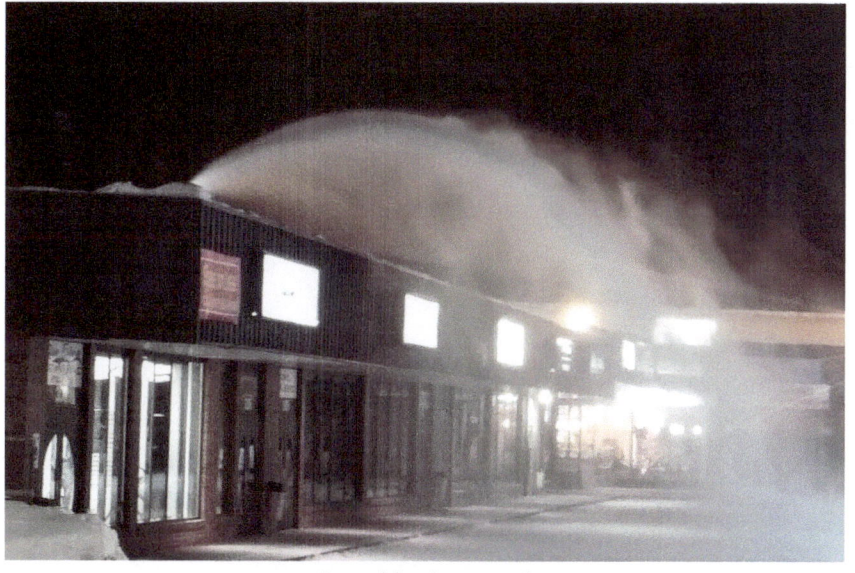

Snow blowing a roof

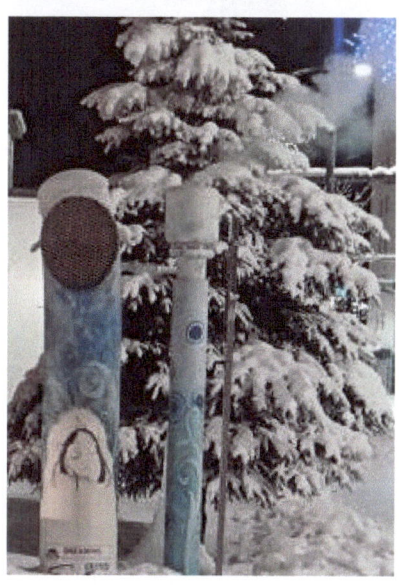

Steam vent for downtown utilidors

Alaska produces some of the most beautiful rainbows I have ever seen

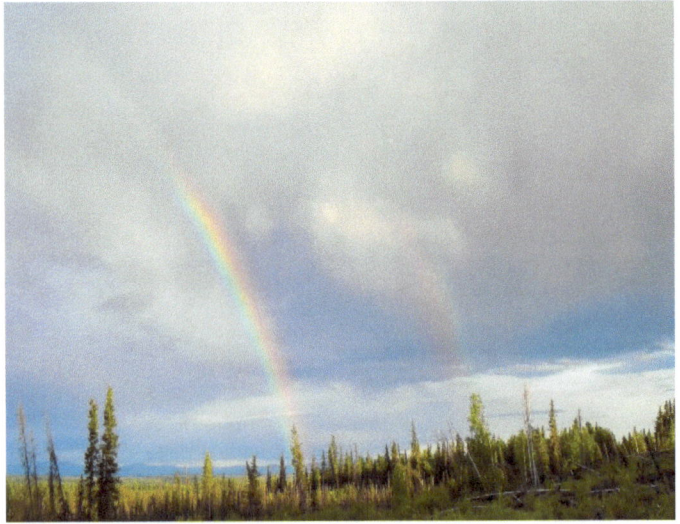

Between Circle City and Central

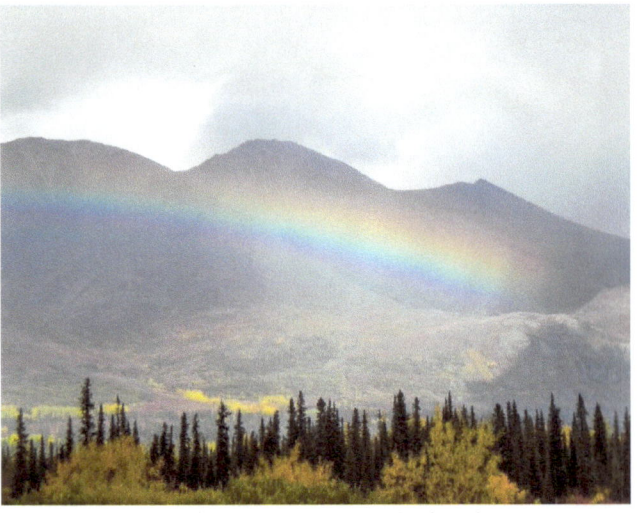

Over the Nenana River north of Healy

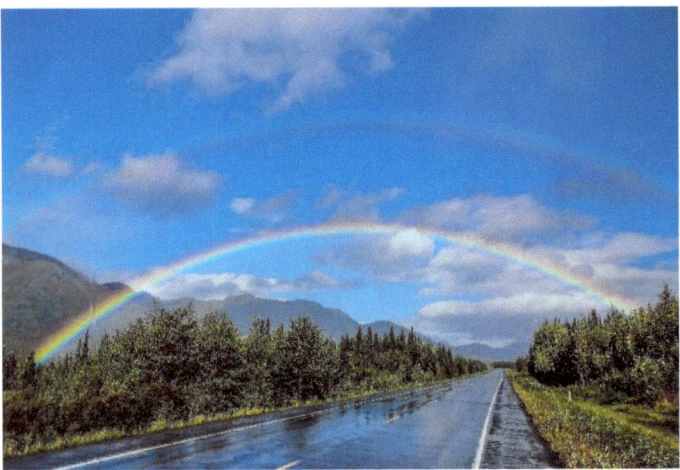

Richardson Highway north of Thompson Pass

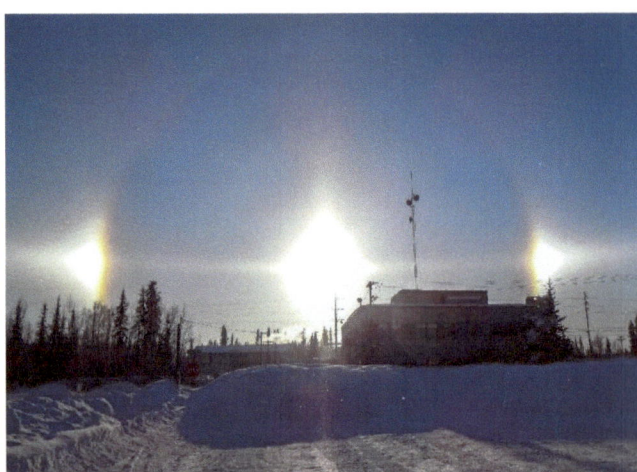

Twin sundogs over Fairbanks

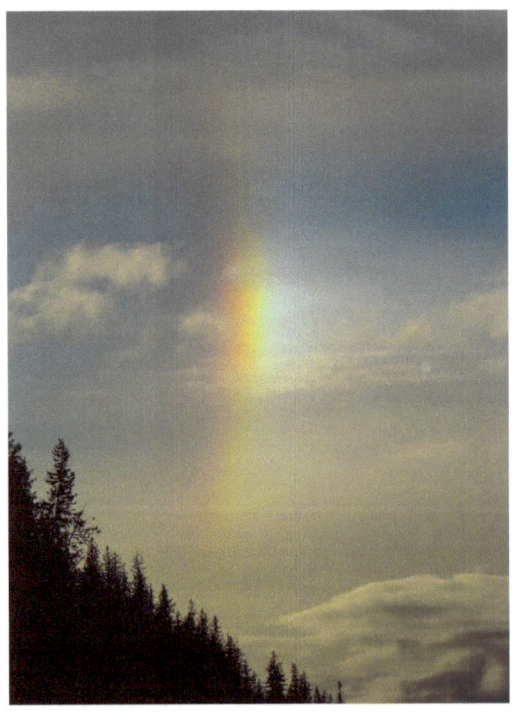

Ice Crystal Sundog over Valdez

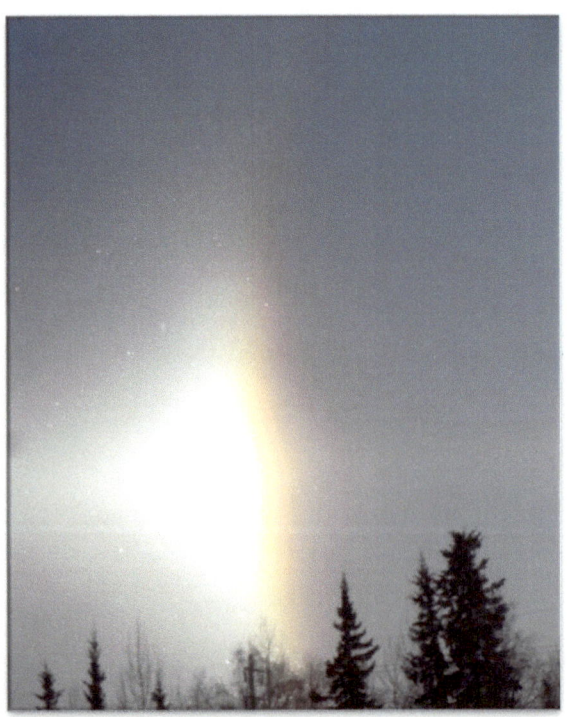

Ice Crystal Sundog over Fairbanks

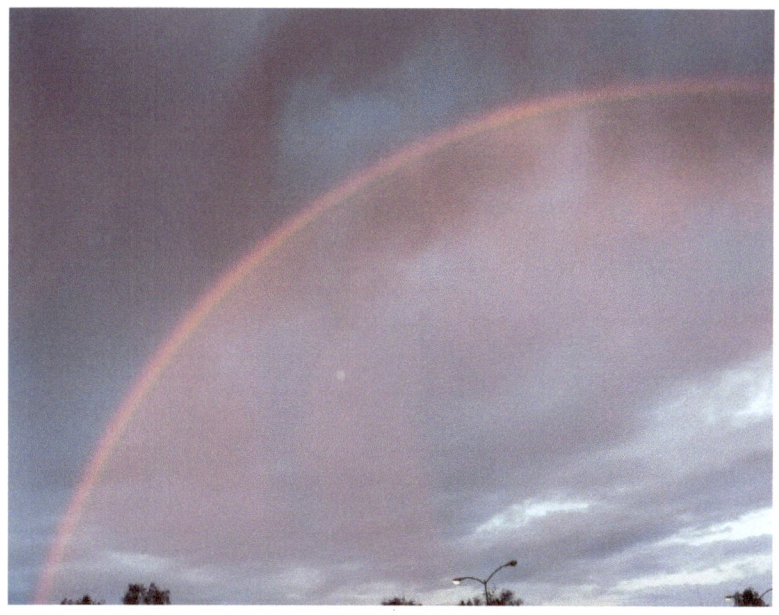

Parks Highway near University of Alaska Fairbanks

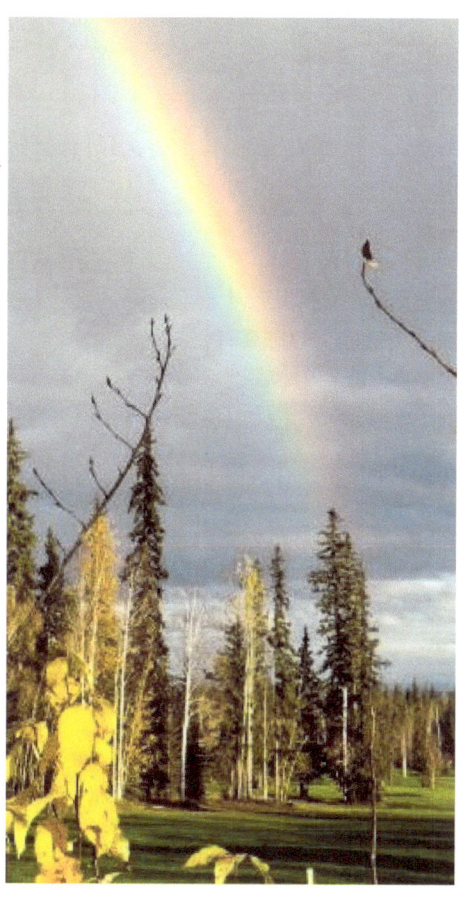

Over Fairbanks golf course

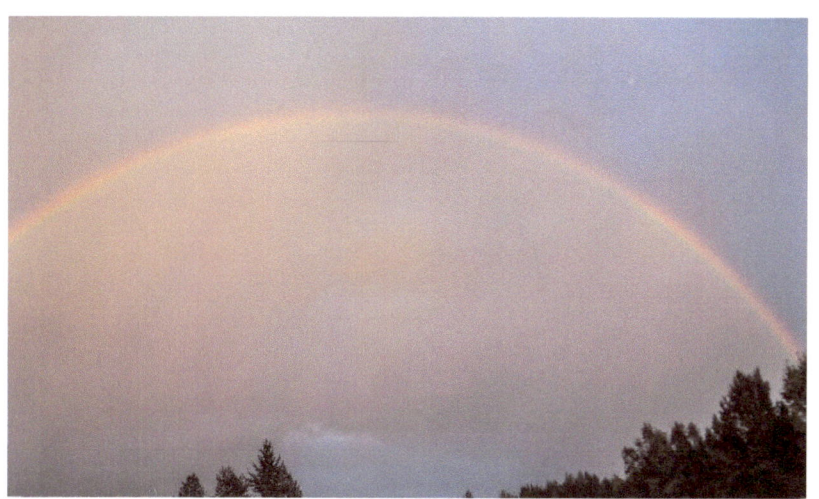

Near Anchorage Airport

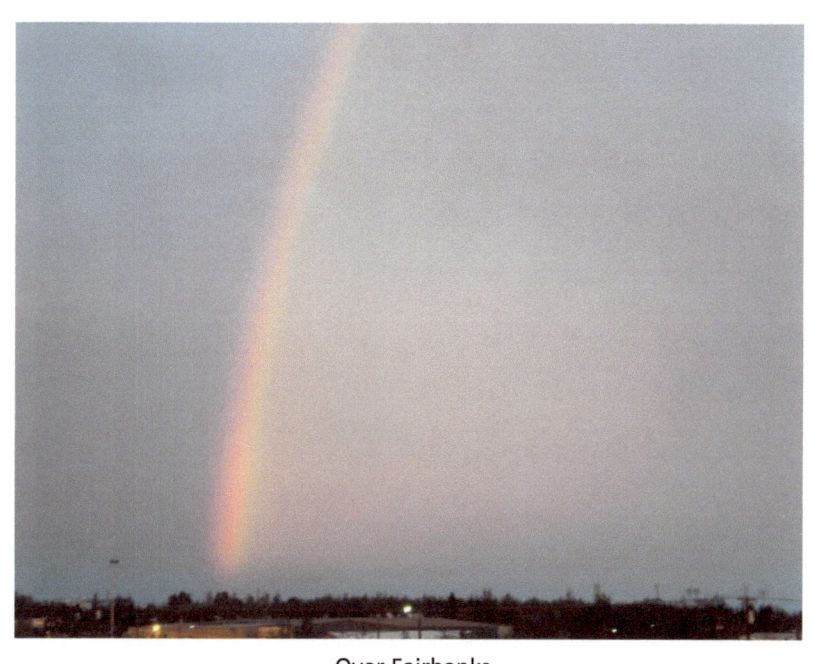

Over Fairbanks

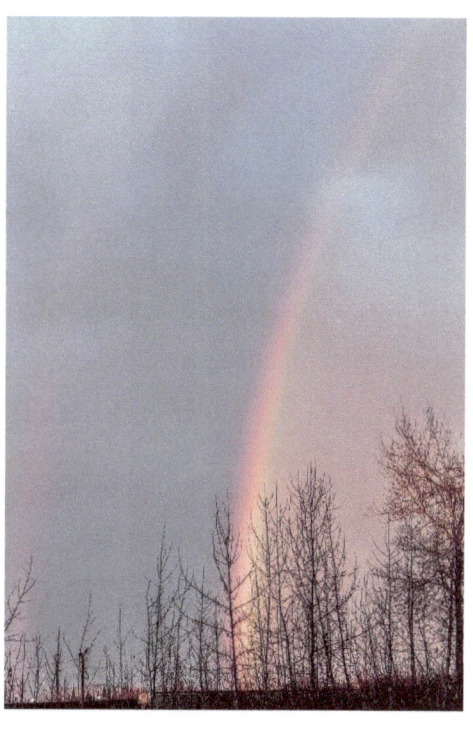

Over Fairbanks rail yard

.....There are bridges on the rivers
As pretty as you please;
But the bow that bridges heaven;
And overtops the trees,
And builds a road from earth to sky,
Is prettier far than these.

(Lines from a poem I learned in childhood – name and author long forgotten)

Heaven's Rainbow

The road across the pass was clear.
The sky above a brilliant blue
and not a cloud was near.
Cept one - small and dark
with veil of mist
Reaching out to touch the earth.
Then, across the road ahead,
An arc of colored light
was gently spread.
From ditch to ditch it arced above
And neath the rainbow arch I drove.
The gentle touch of heaven's hand
In that multi-colored band
A sense of awe swept over me
A depth of peace no words can tell
When He reaches out from heaven
where He and angels dwell.

26

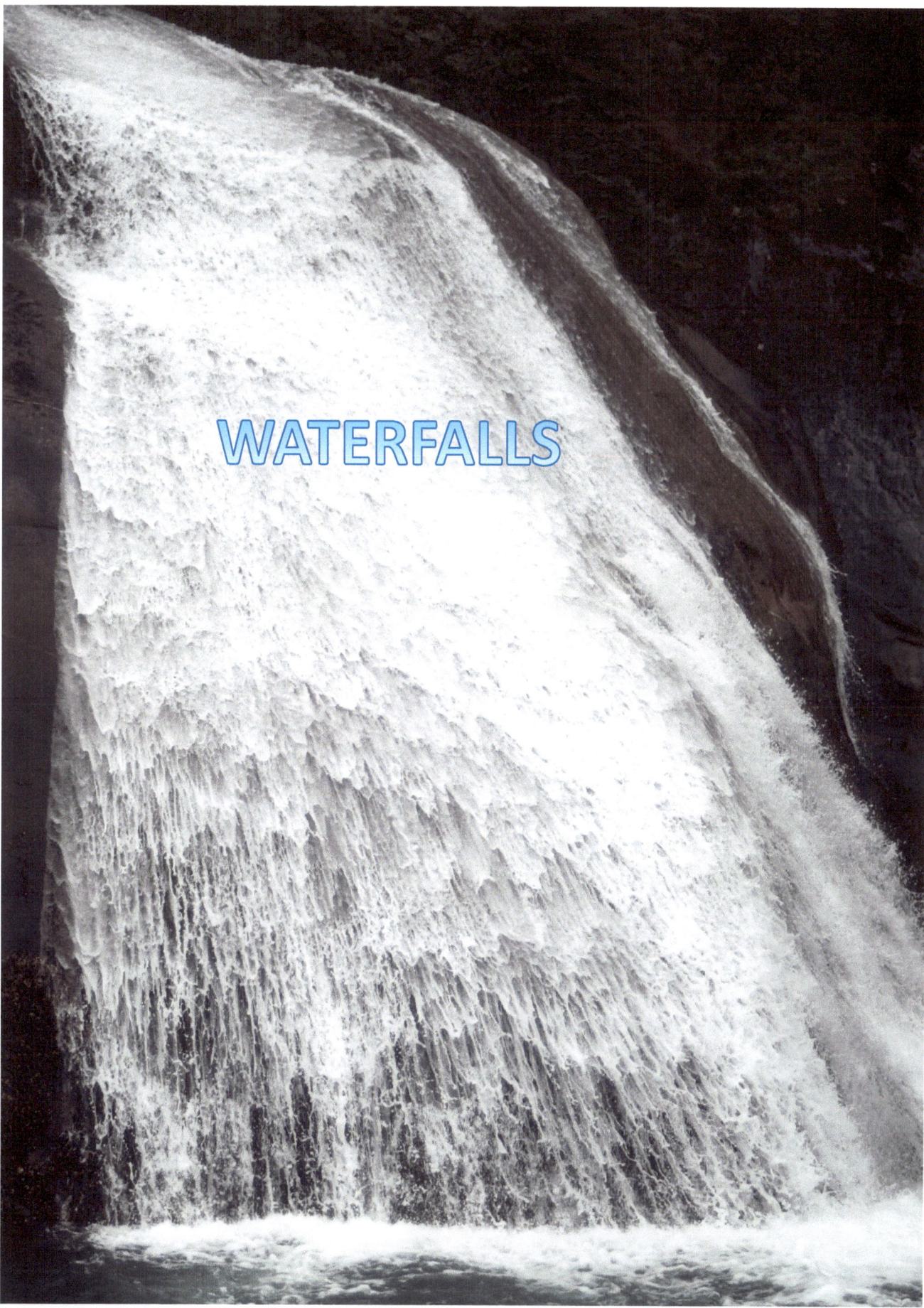

WATERFALLS

Keystone Canyon

Valdez

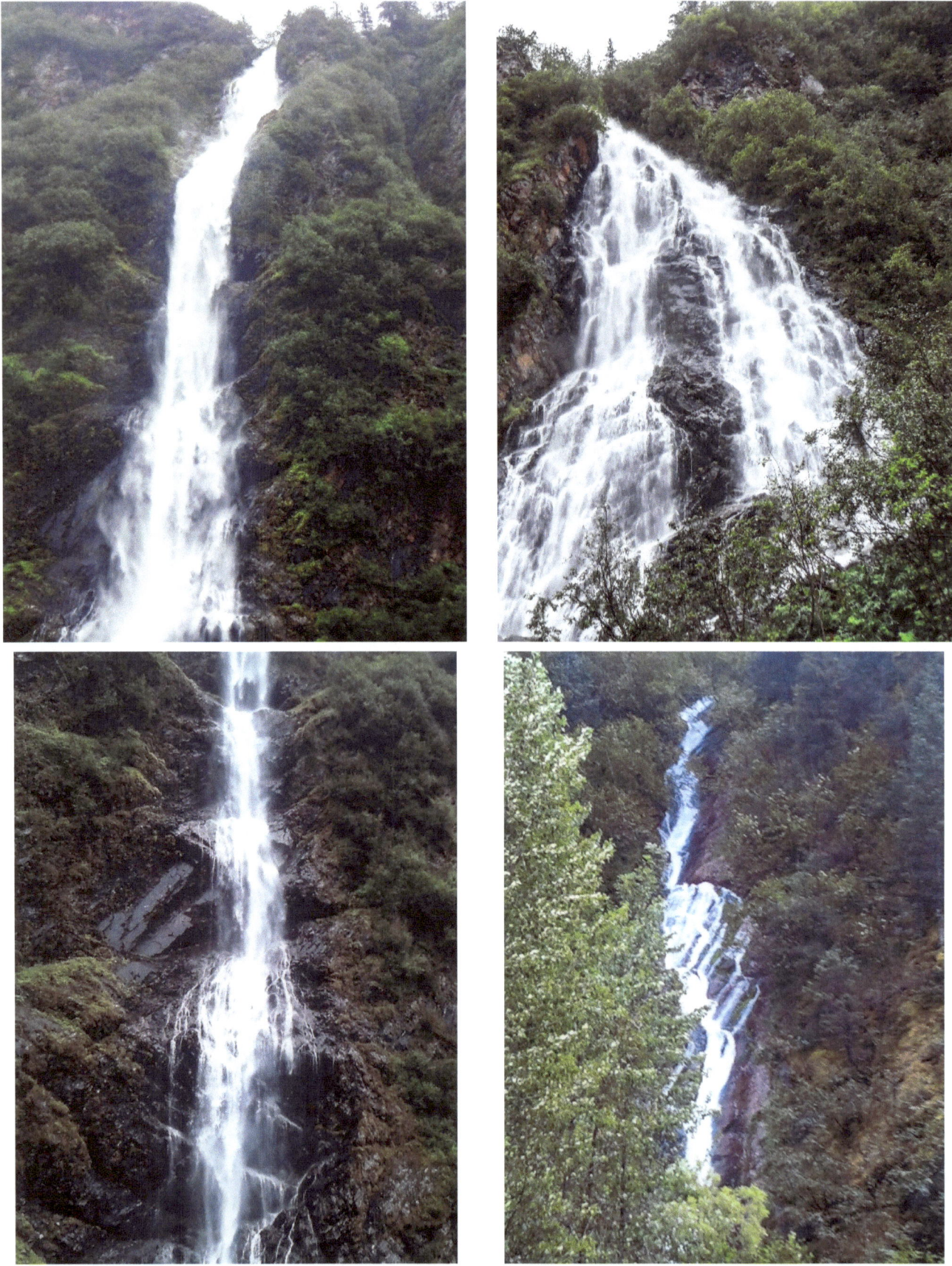

Tracy Arm Waterfalls

Juneau

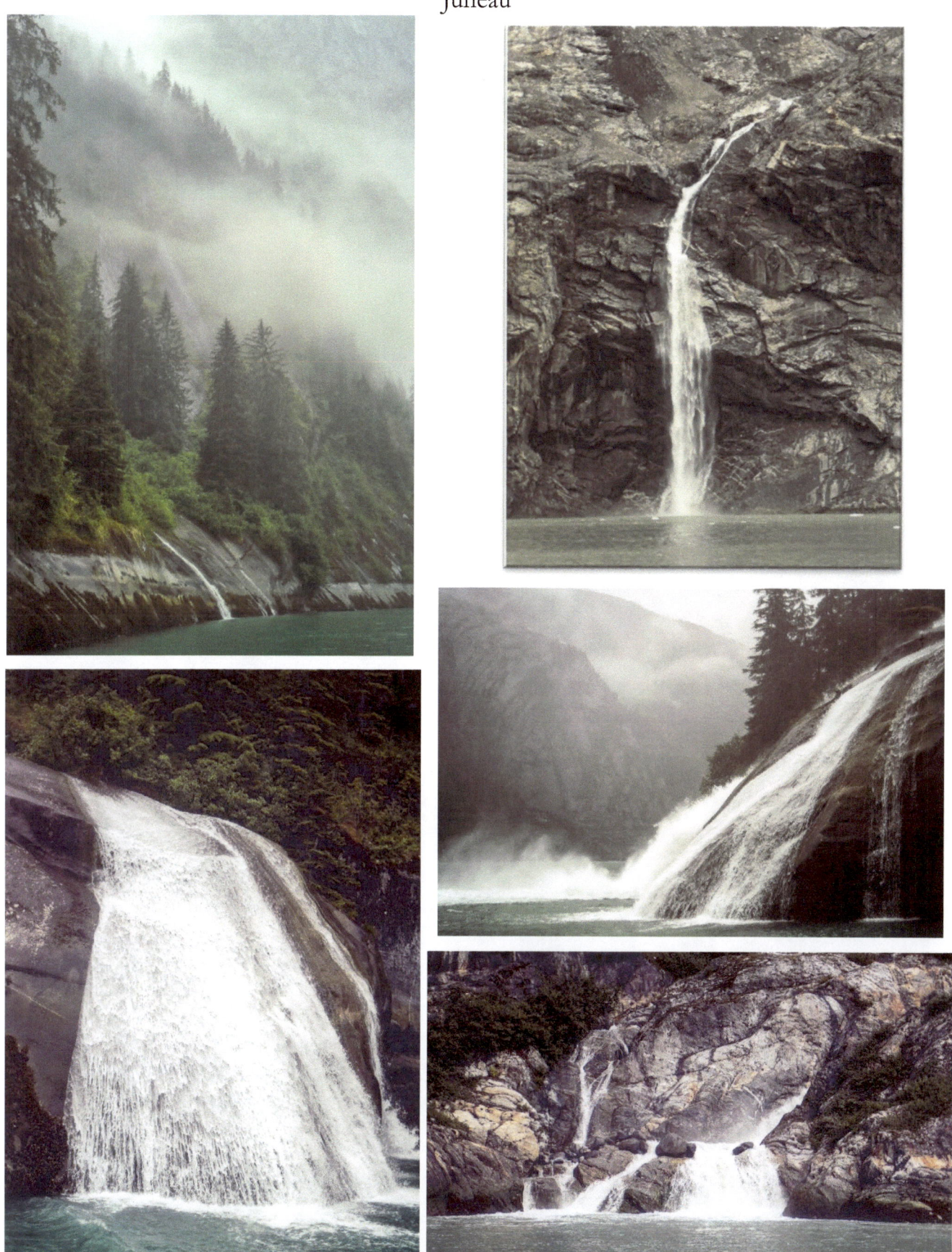

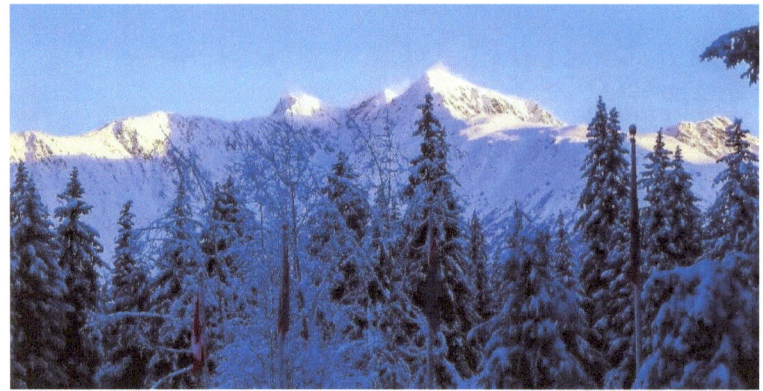

Alyeska Resort - Girdwood

Alaska Sunrise

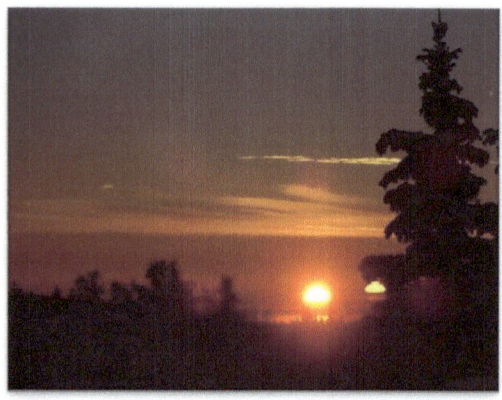

Off Farmer's Loop - Fairbanks

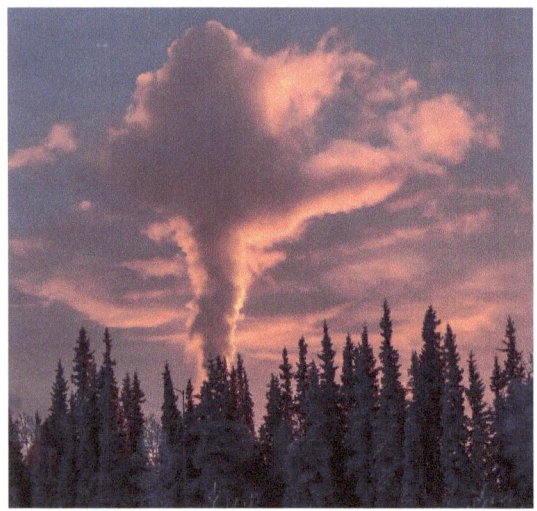

Power plant plume from Danby - Fairbanks

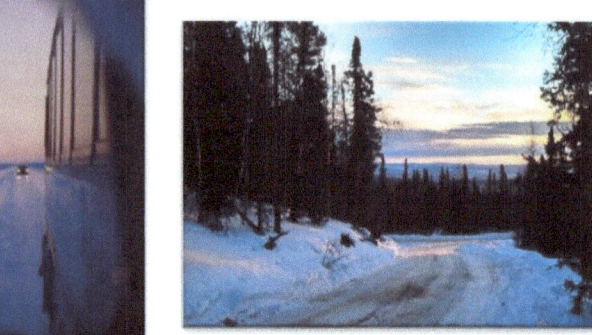

On the Beaufort Sea

Sunrise from Moose Mountain

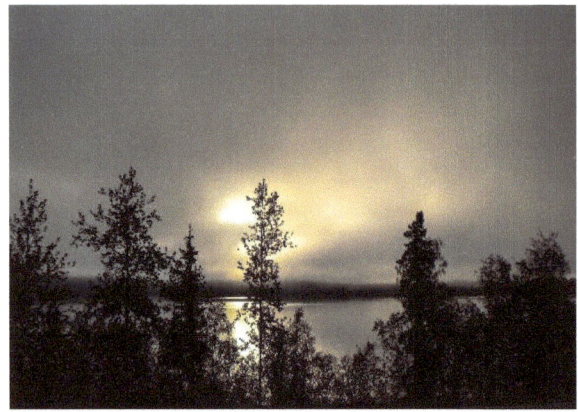

Sunrise over Harding Lake

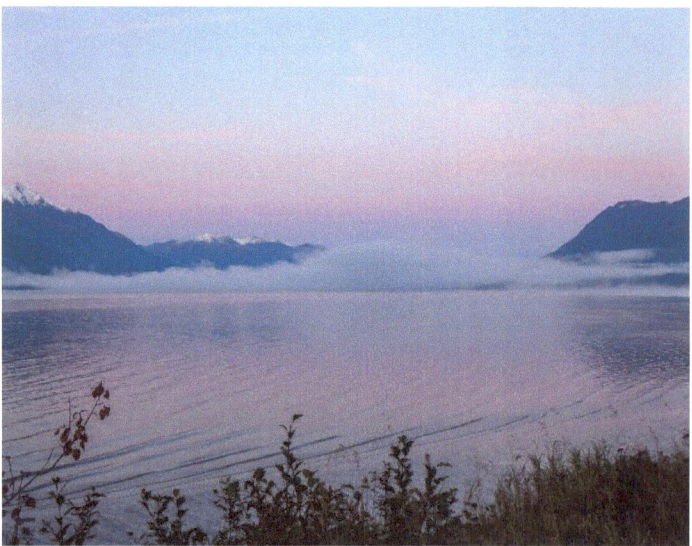

Sunrise over Turnagain Arm

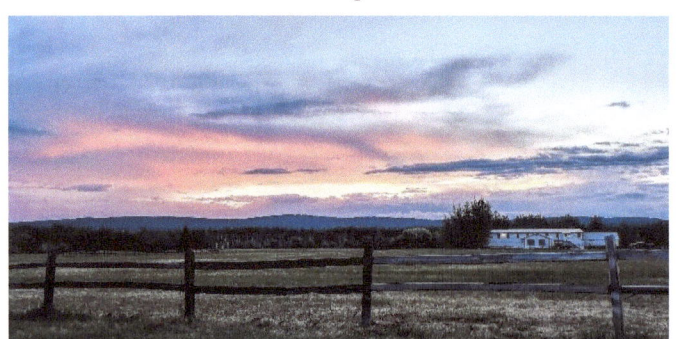

Sunrise over Creamers Dairy - Fairbanks

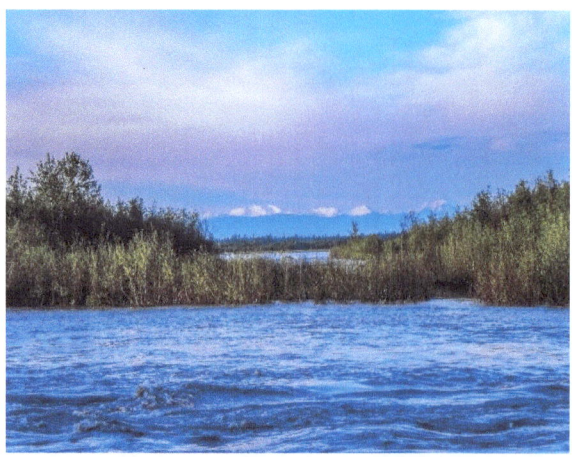

Sunrise over Tanana River at Delta

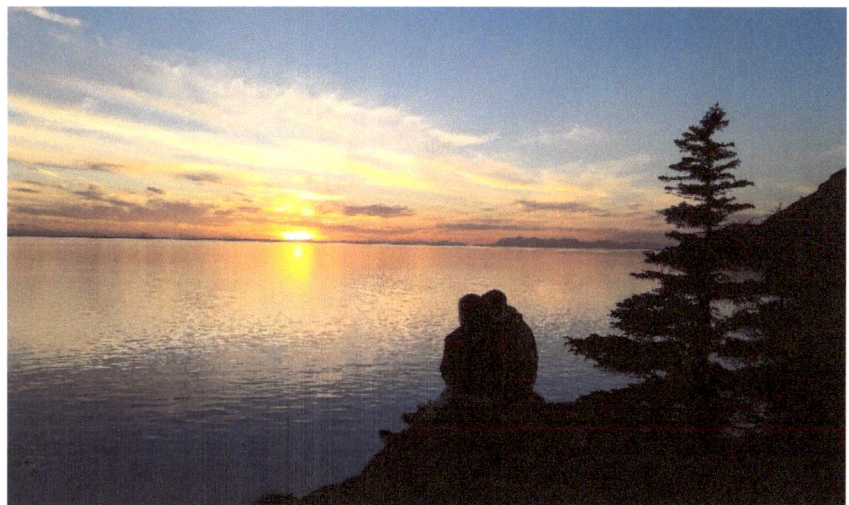

Sunset over Turnagain Arm

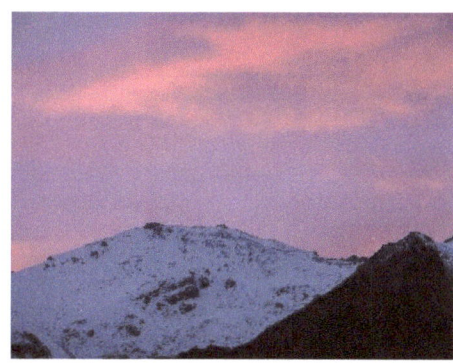

Sunset from McKinley Chalet – Denali Park

Alaska Sunset

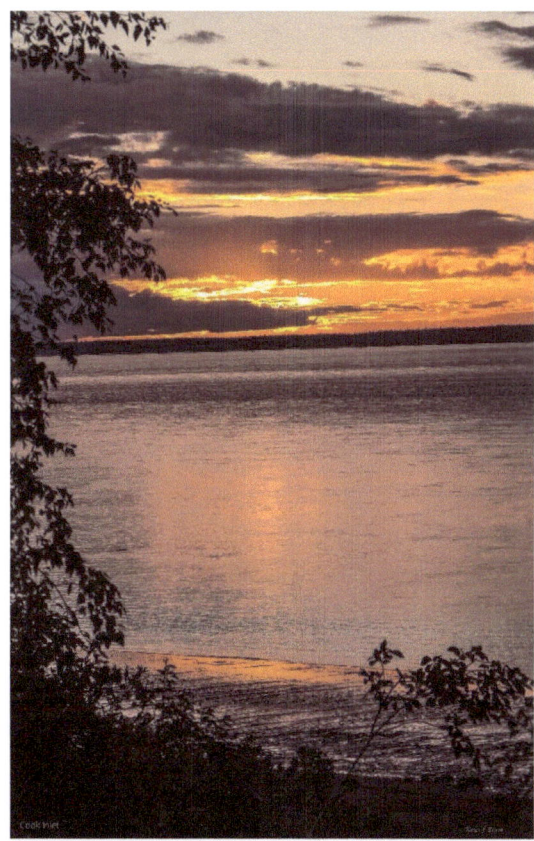

Sunset over Cook Inlet

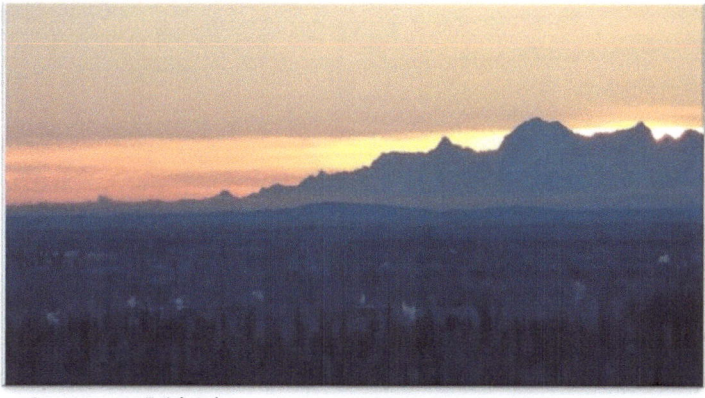

Sunset over Fairbanks

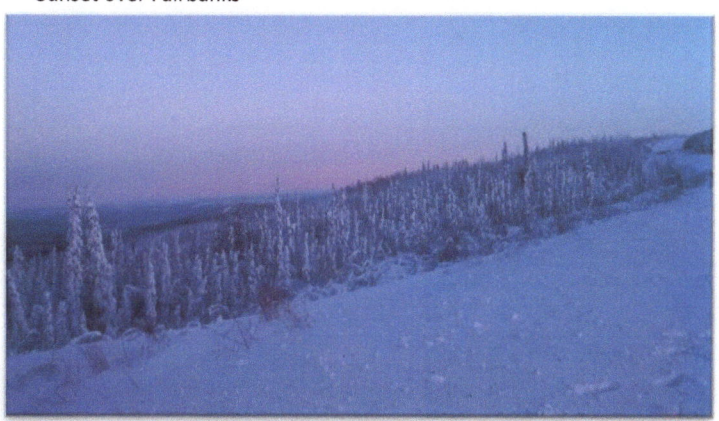

Sunset off the Dalton Highway

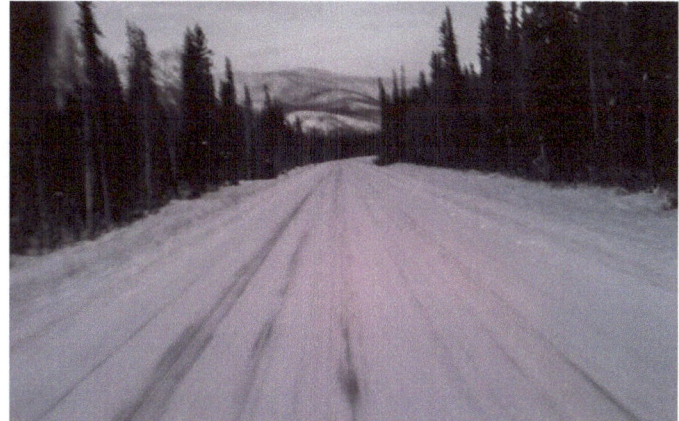

Chena Hot Springs Road

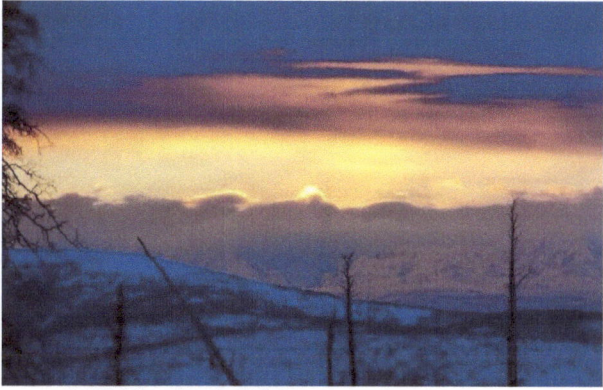

Pogo Mine Road -Delta

A GLIMPSE OF ALASKA WILDLIFE

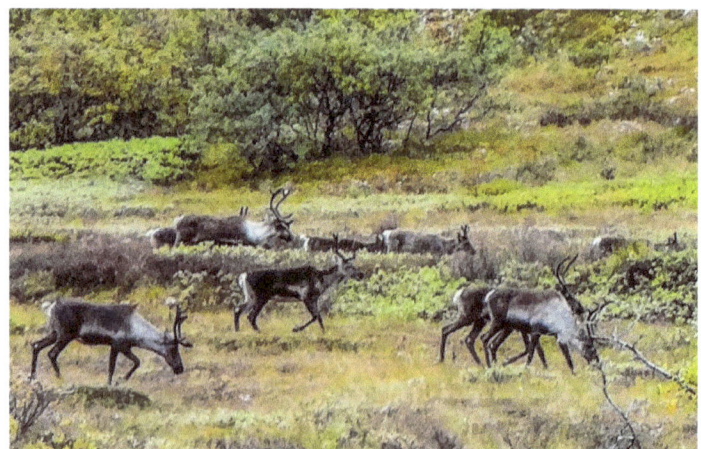

Denali Caribou

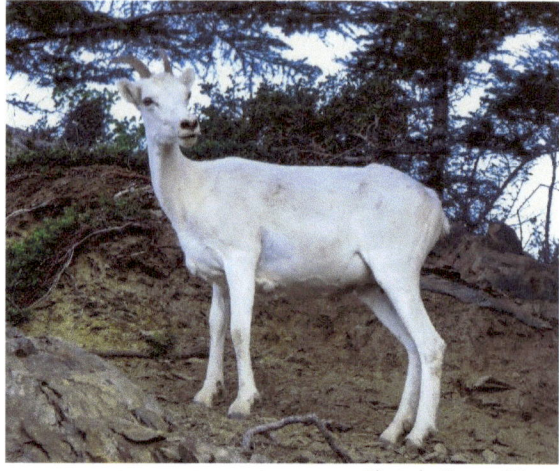

Mountain Goat – Seward Hwy   Photo by Howard Hess

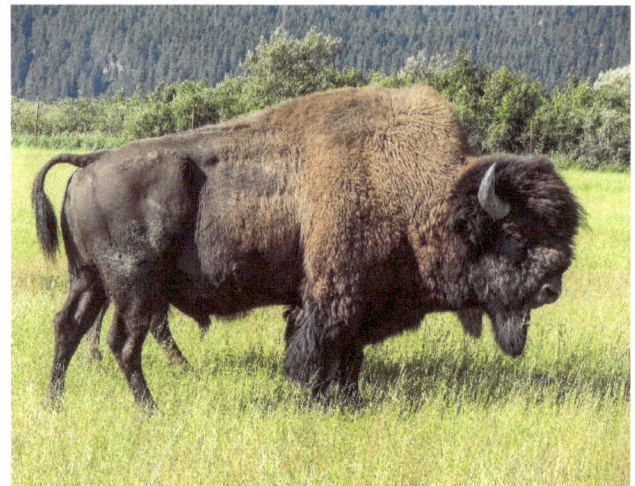

Wood Bison - Portage

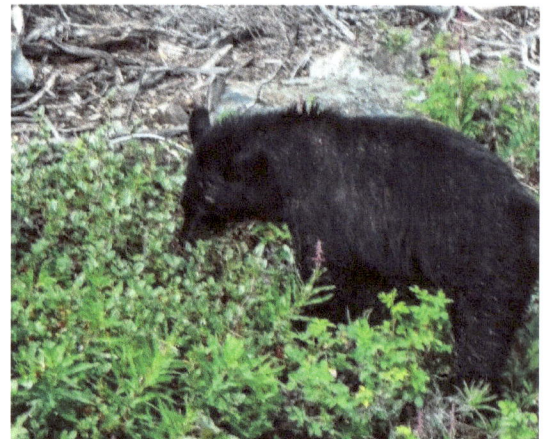

Black Bear South Klondike Hwy

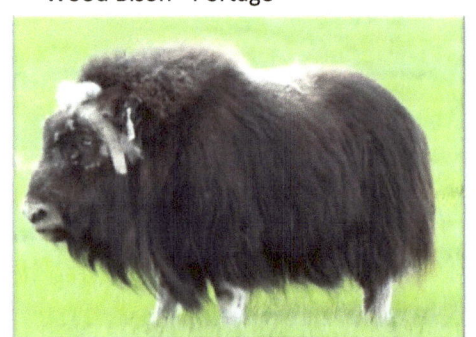

Musk Ox - Palmer

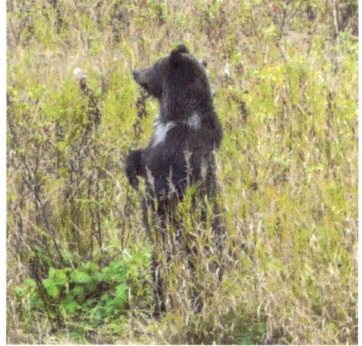

Curious Cub - Haines

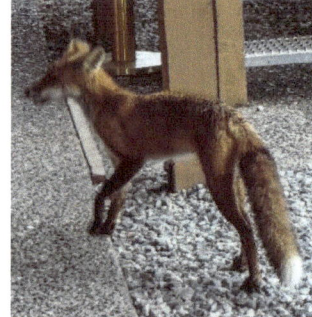

Talkeetna Fox

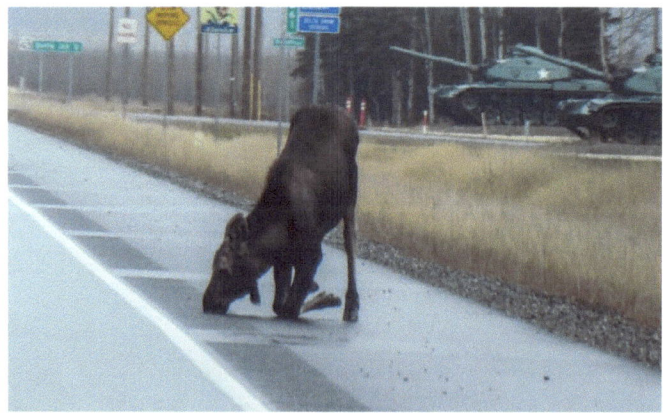

Moose near Delta – Licking salt

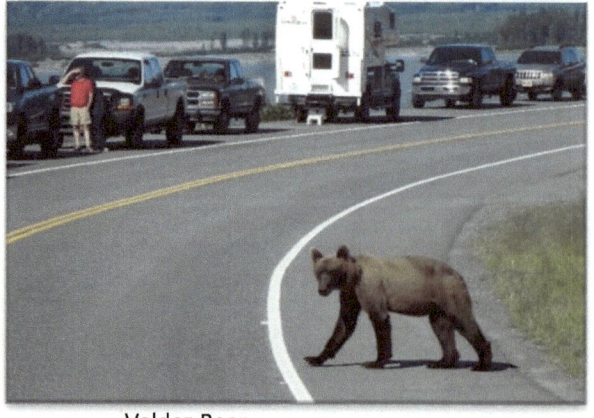

Valdez Bear

Visitors to Alaska expect to see wildlife, the mountain (Denali) and some expect it to be cold and snowy - even in summer (and sometimes they get to witness an unseasonal snowstorm!). Alaska is a bit larger than the three largest states combined with a total population less than Fort Worth, Texas. With 663,268 sq. miles, there is plenty of space for wildlife, but as Alaska's population grows, communities expand, population spreads out, roads thread into the wilderness, traffic increases, noise level rises and all of it pushes the animals further into the wilderness – away from people, vehicles of all kinds on and off the road, aircraft and noise pollution.

Texas - 268,581 sq. mi   California - 163,696 sq. mi   Montana - 147,040 sq. mi
Ft. Worth, Texas pop - 895,008

There's plenty of wildlife: the largest bald eagle population in the nation, the Porcupine Caribou herd has the longest migration of any land mammal in the world; home to 98% of the U.S. brown bear population (70% of the North American) – considered to be the largest carnivorous land mammal alive today. Exact animal counts are hard to get but, the bear population in Alaska is estimated at 30,000 brown bears and as many as 100,000 black bears. The grizzly count, at about 40,000 is 40 times higher than the rest of the U.S. A 2016 study of Polar bears showed about 2,937 bears in the Chukchi Sea region with an estimated Southern Beaufort Sea subpopulation (shared with Canada) adding another 2,500.

Thirtytwo caribou herds wander the tundra and forests of Alaska with an estimated combined population of around 750,000 animals. Moose, found pretty much all over the state, number 175,000 to 200,000. Weighing up to 1,600 pounds, Alaska-Yukon moose are the largest of the eight subspecies of moose. Antlers are the fastest growing tissue in any mammal and adding a pound of bone and an inch a day a bull can grow an 80 lb. rack in one summer.

Alaska's wood bison were hunted to extinction but were reintroduced from a northern Canadian herd. The only U.S. free roaming herd is located along the Innoko River in Southwest Alaska where there is little chance the herd of 120 – 130 animals will intermingle with the plains bison in the Delta area which now number about 900.

Hunted to near worldwide extinction, the total population of musk ox is estimated at 125,000 animals. Reintroduced to Alaska from Greenland in 1935, there are now about 2,300 scattered in small herds on Nunivak and Nelson Islands, the Seward Peninsula, the Yukon-Kuskokwim Delta, northwest Alaska, north central Alaska and northeast Alaska.

Dall sheep, the northern most species of wild sheep in North America, numbered about 45,000 statewide in 2010. The western Brooks Range is the edge of the North American range for this alpine dweller. Mountain goats are found in the coastal areas of southeast and southcentral Alaska. The least studied large mammal in North America, they number about 24,000 – 33,500 in the state.

Between 7,000 to 11,000 wolves roam 85% of Alaska. Although there are two recognized subspecies, wolves from the Interior are probably descendants of those that inhabited Beringia during the ice age. As ice melted, wolves from the western U.S. followed black tail deer north along the coast to Southeast Alaska where wolves today are not only darker and smaller, but genetically different from northern wolves.

If you are a bird watcher, there are over 430 species of birds in Alaska.

Alaska - 663,268 sq. miles   Anchorage – 5,035 sq. mi   Fairbanks – 33.sq. mi   Juneau 3,225 sq. mi
Alaska State population - 710,249   Anchorage – 385,000   Fairbanks: 31,516   Juneau – 32,164

There's a lot of land for wildlife; a lot of square miles for each animal with little to no chance of encountering people and noise. Animal population is regulated by food and water availability as well as climatic conditions, predator numbers and disease. Animal viewing depends on population density, weather conditions, time of day, traffic and pure luck. They have a routine, seasons to live by and a life that is not dictated by man alone. Waiting on the side of the road for tourists to arrive with camera in hand is just not a top priority for them!

Whale Watching

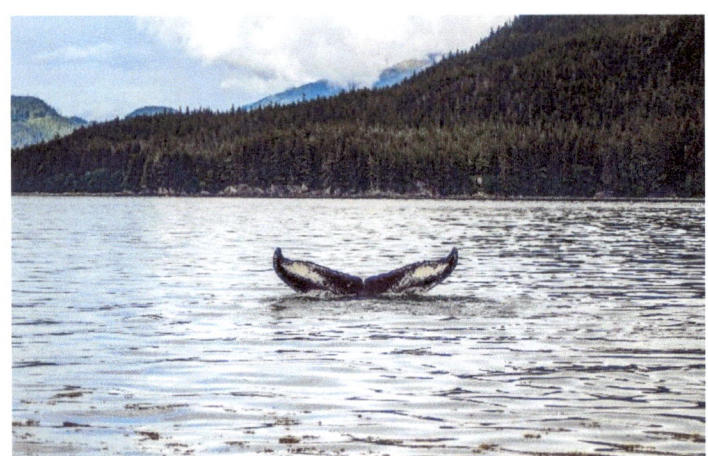
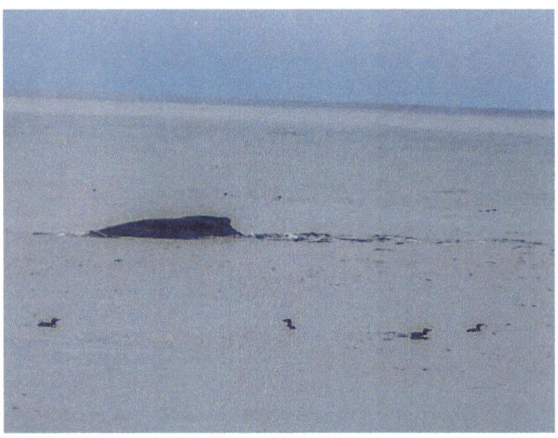
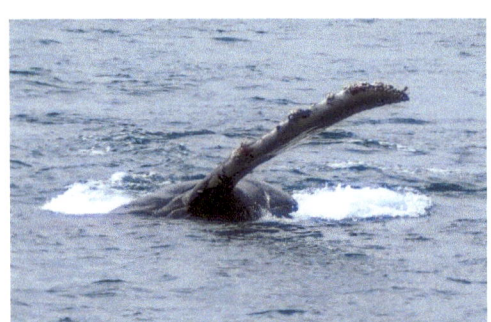
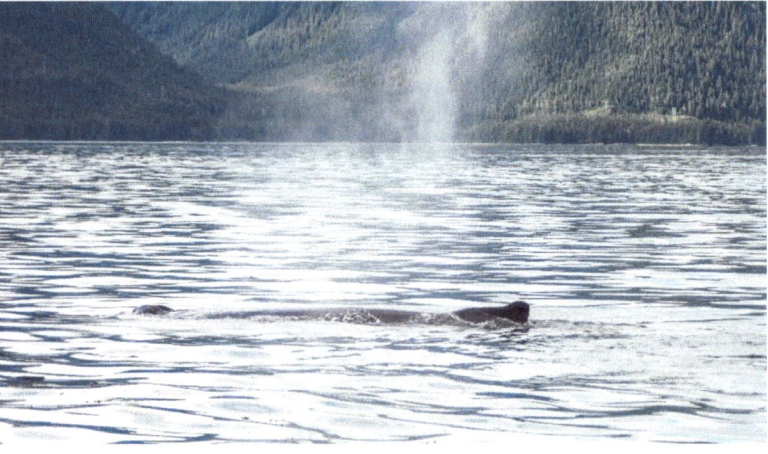
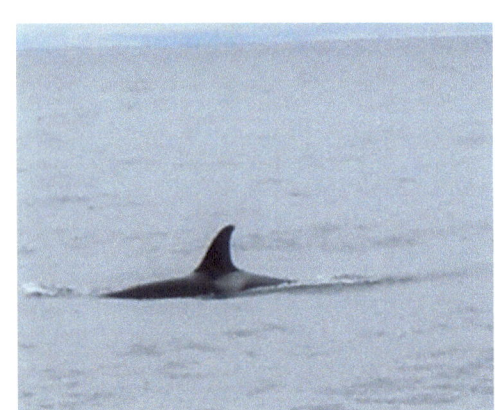
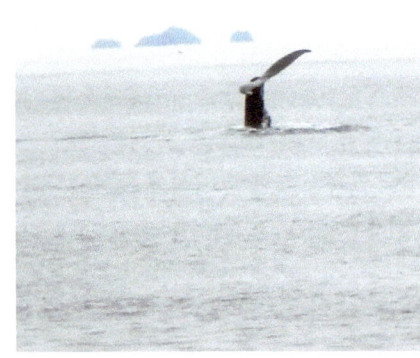
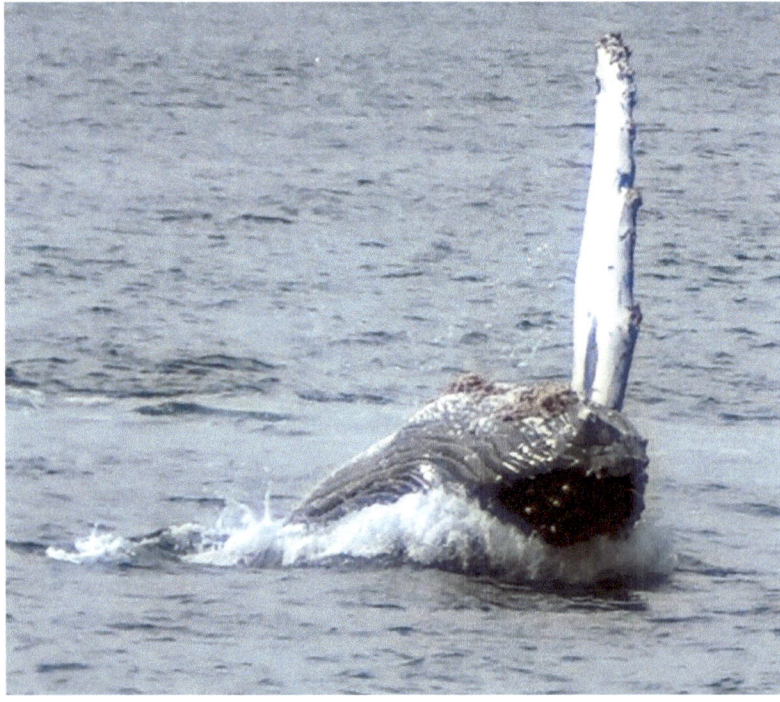

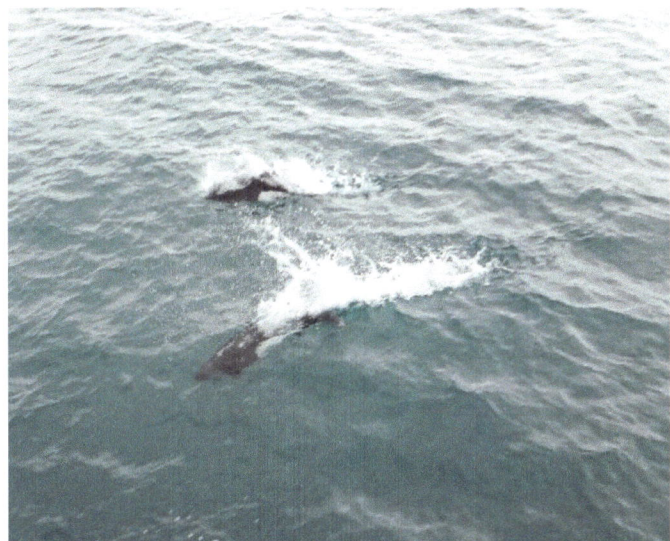

Dall Porpoise – Gulf of Alaska

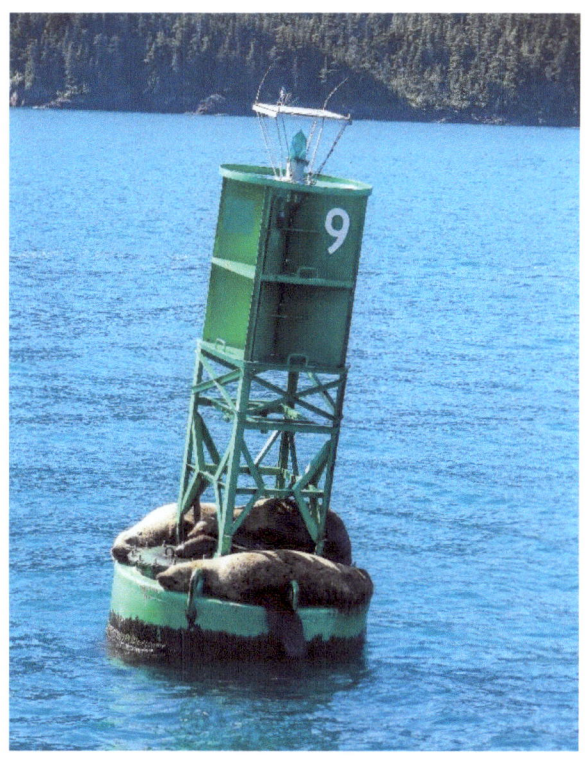

Harbor Seals – Resurrection Bay

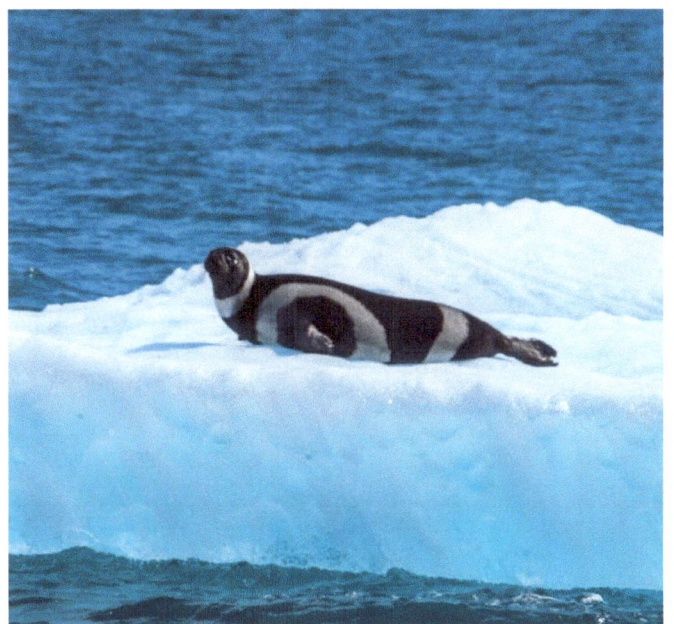

Ringed Seal – Gulf of Alaska

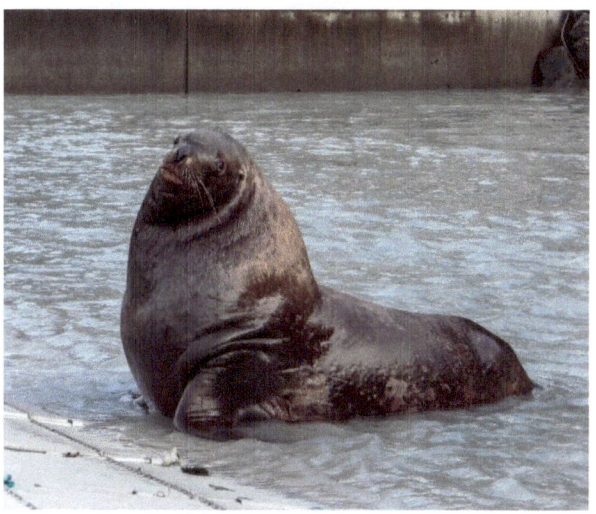

Sea Lion - Valdez

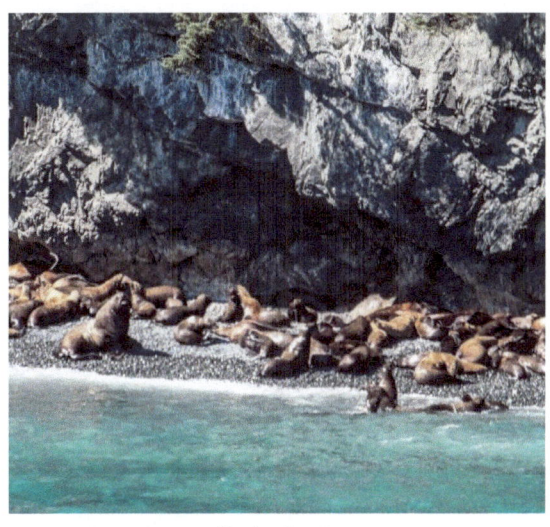

Sea Lions off Alaska Coast

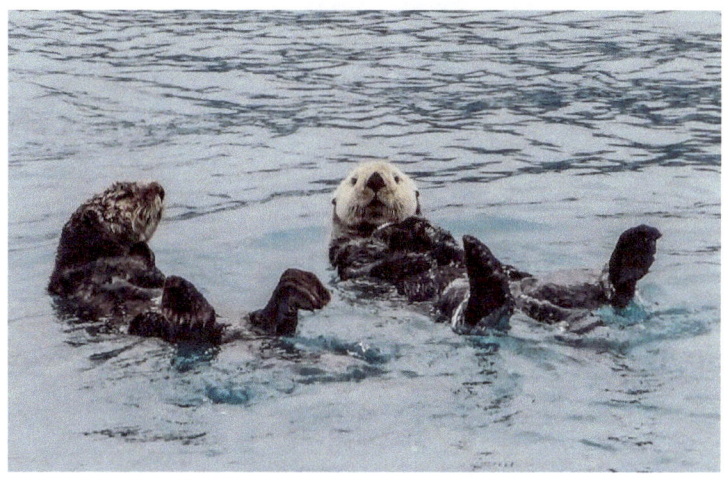

Resurrection Bay Sea Otters

Bird Watching

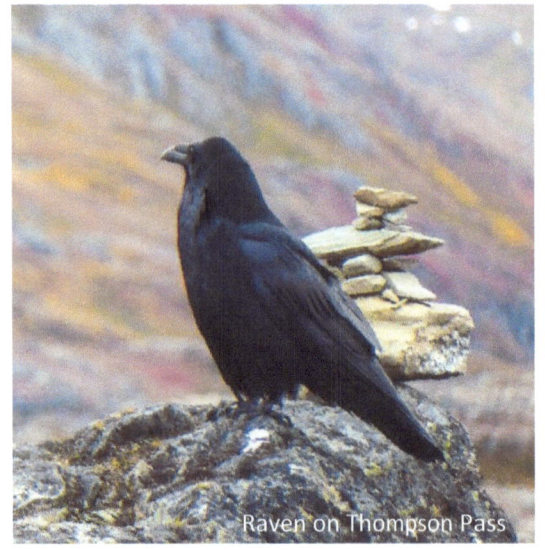

Raven on Thompson Pass

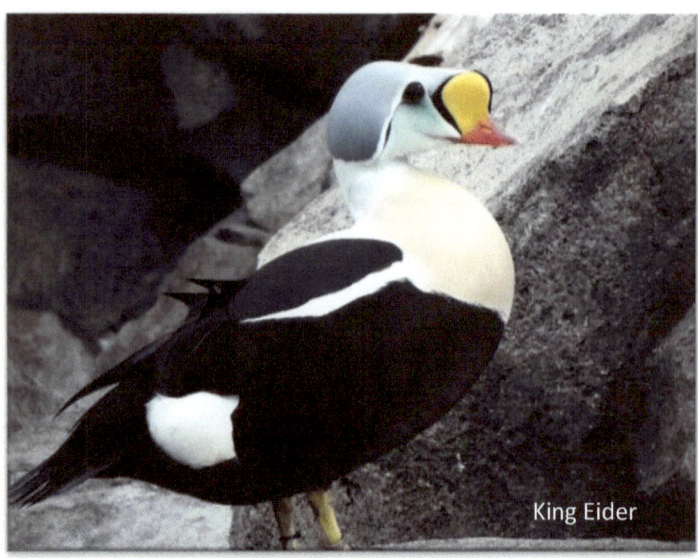

King Eider

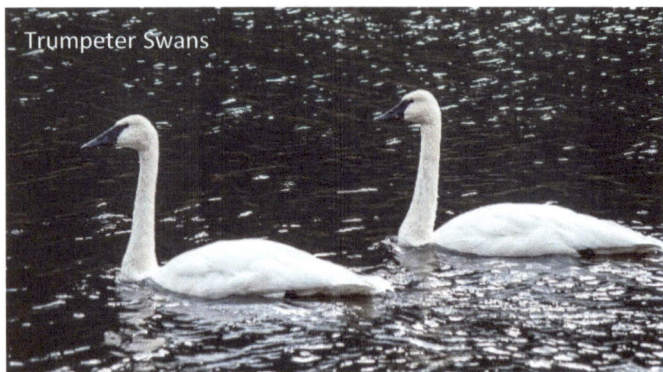

Trumpeter Swans

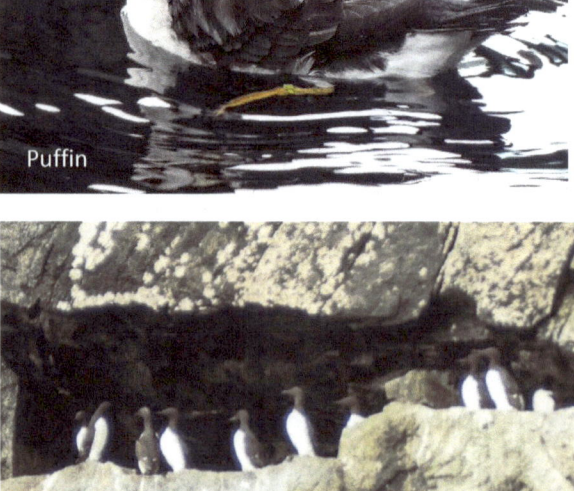

Puffin

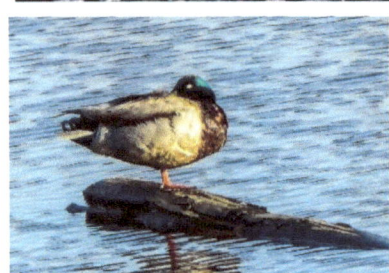

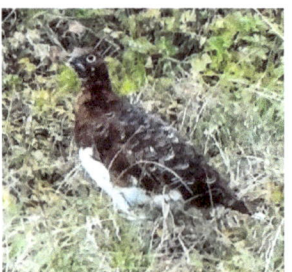

Teal Duck

Willow Ptarmigan

Muirs

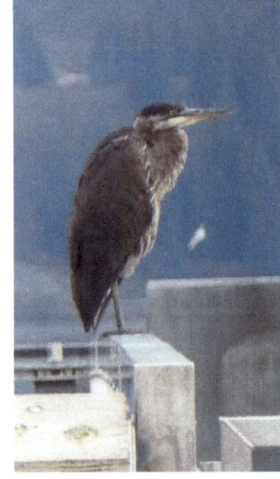

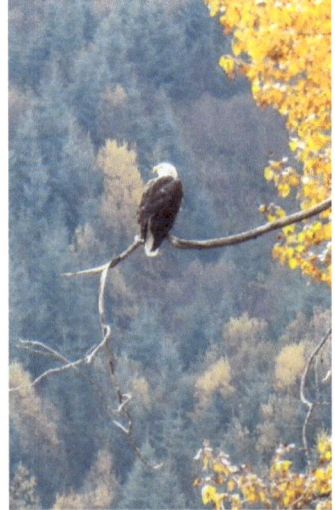

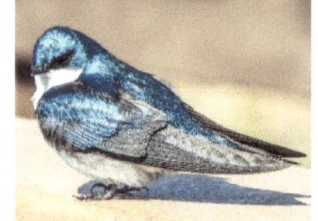

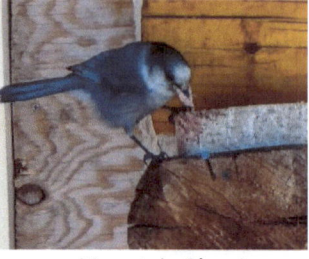

Great Blue Heron

Eagle - Haines

Tree Swallow

Mountain Blue Jay

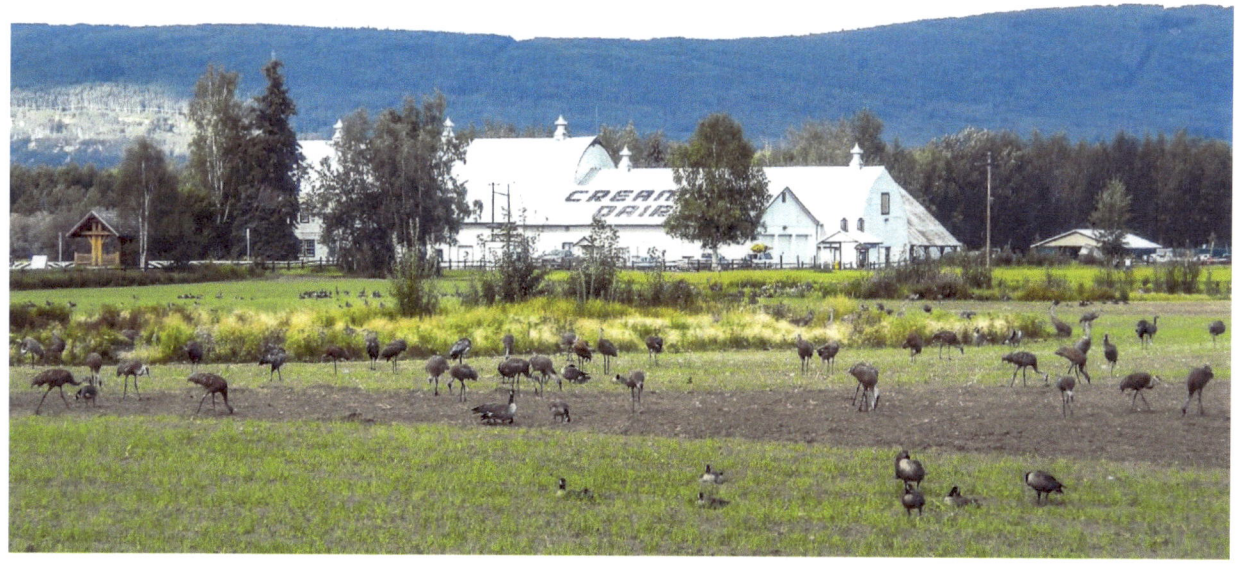

Migratory Birds at Creamers Field in Fairbanks

Creamers Dairy in Fairbanks dates back to the gold rush days when it was a very successful dairy. Established in 1904 and moved to its present location in 1915, the dairy produced milk, buttermilk, cottage cheese whipping cream, ice cream, sherbet, chocolate milk, and even a non-dairy orange drink until the early 1950s. The dairy closed in 1966 and Fairbanks residents purchased the property to ensure the return of the flocks of migratory birds. Volunteers prepare the fields in early spring for the eagerly awaited return of over 100 species of birds headed north to nesting areas. Alaska's arctic coastal plain is one of the most productive wetland nesting grounds in the world. Each spring, millions of birds migrate here from wintering grounds in nearly every part of the globe. For many birds, Alaska is the beginning point for migratory routes they will use during their entire lifetime. Alaska birds migrate to six continents, but the longest nonstop bird migration in the world is that of the Bar-Tailed Godwit from Alaska to New Zealand.

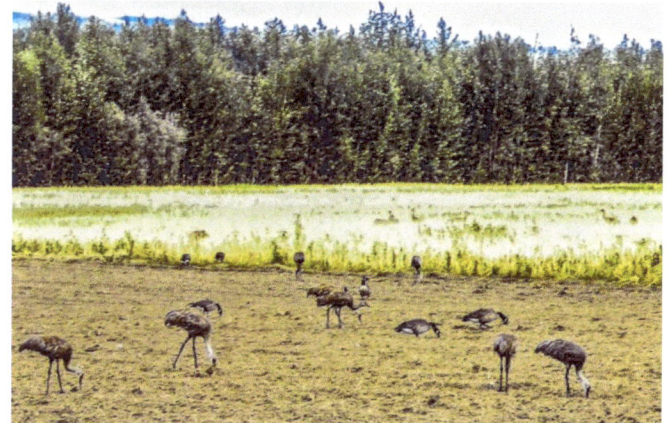

Sandhill Cranes

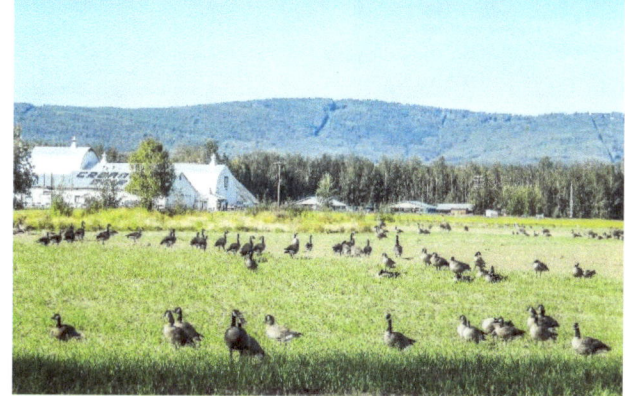

Canada Geese

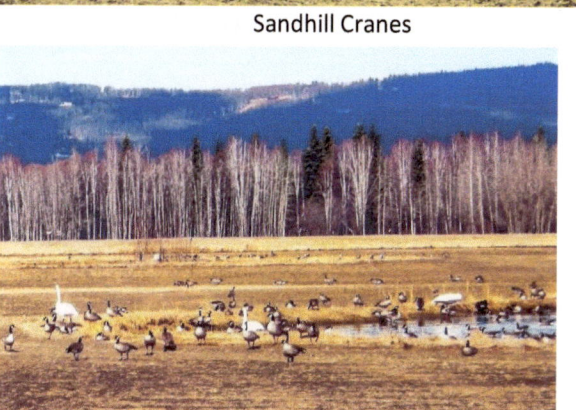

Swans and Geese

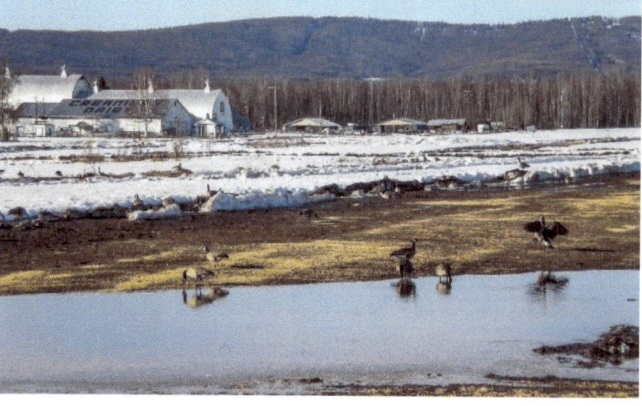

Alaska Flowers

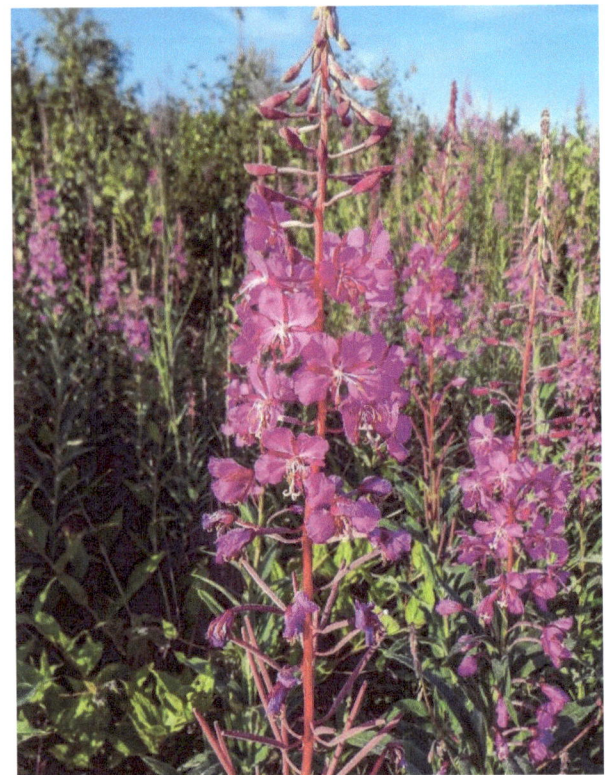

Fireweed

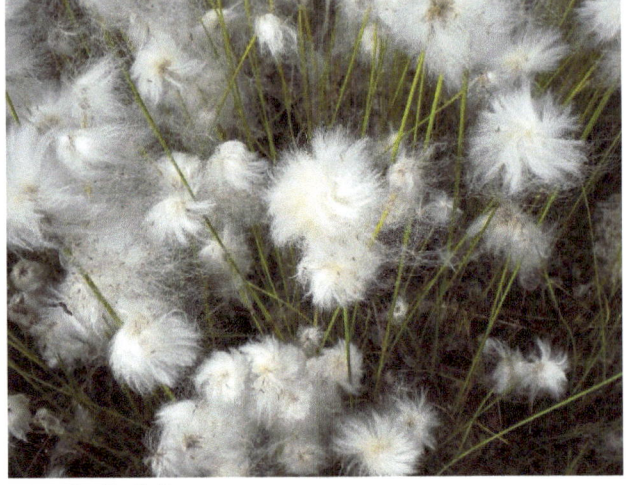

Arctic Cotton

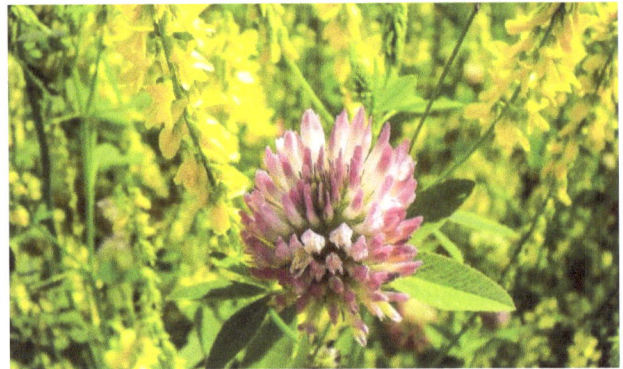

White Sweet Clover

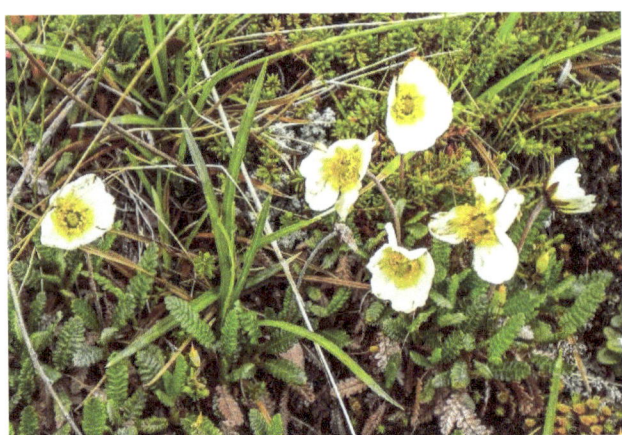

Mountain Avens

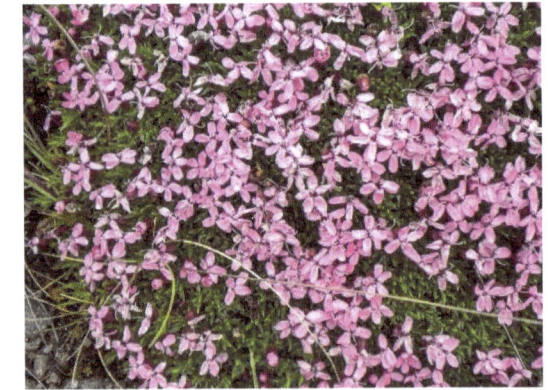

Moss Campion – Eagle Summit

Alaska
Wild Rose
Tanana River

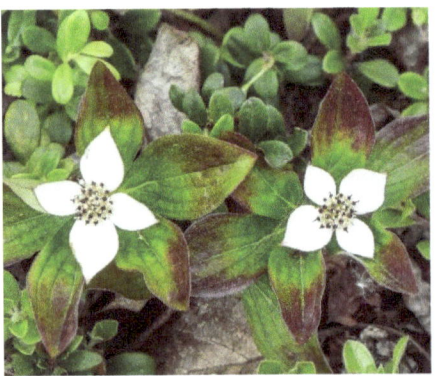

Dwarf Dogwood

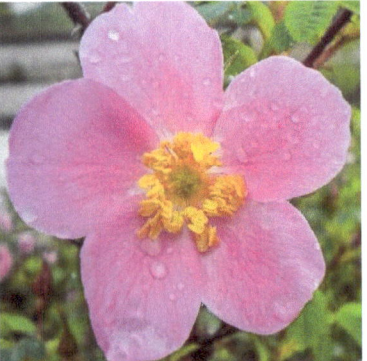

Karen in a field of fireweed

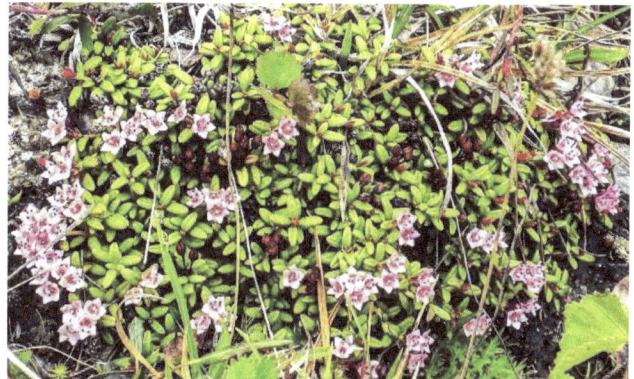
Alpine Azaleas

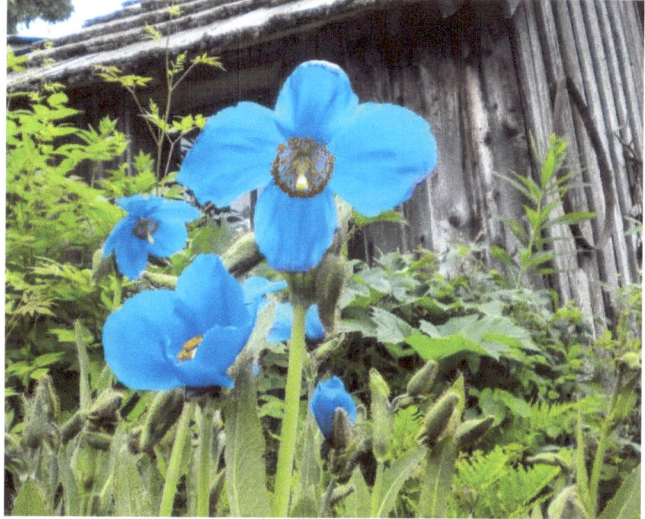
Himalayan Poppies

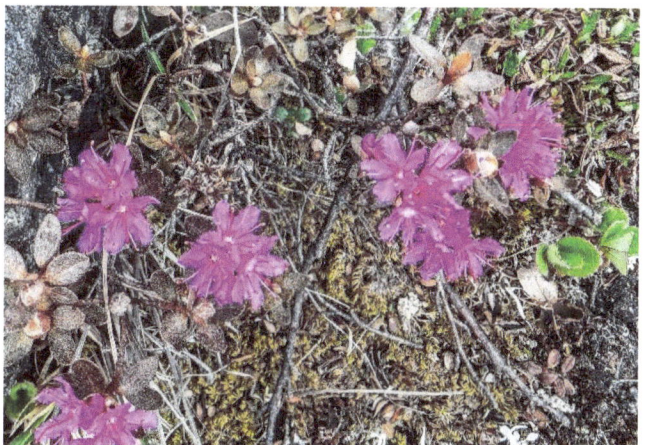
Lapland Rhododendron

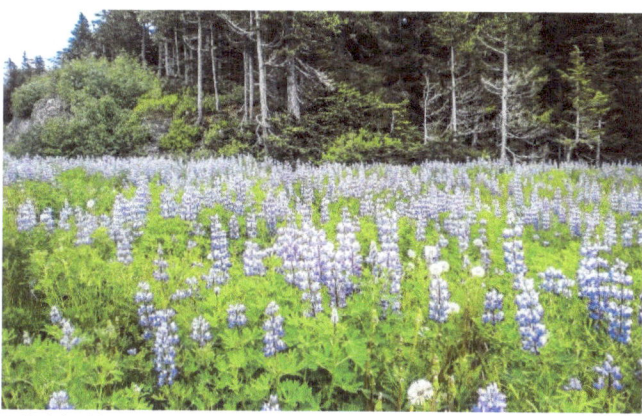
A field of lupine near Seward

Daylight and temperature combine to create brilliant depths of color and large sizes in Alaska's flowers. The optimum temperature for blooming plants is about 62° - the average Alaska temperature. Alaska plants don't have to waste much energy cooling down – instead, energy is spent creating deep brilliant colors. Size is attributable to exposure to 24 hour daylight.

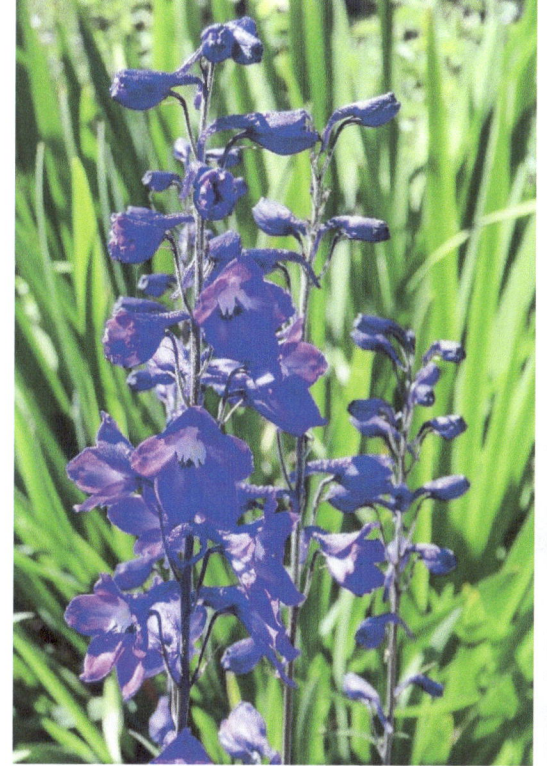
Harebell

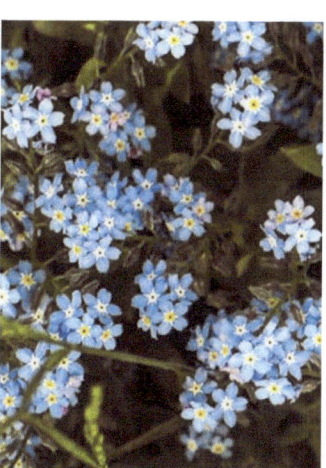
For-get-me- not

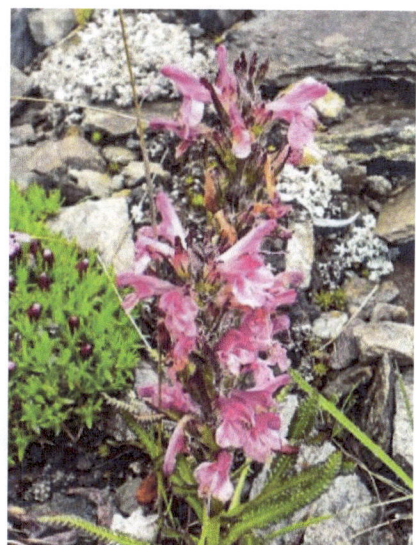
Arctic Lousewort

WINTER DRIVING

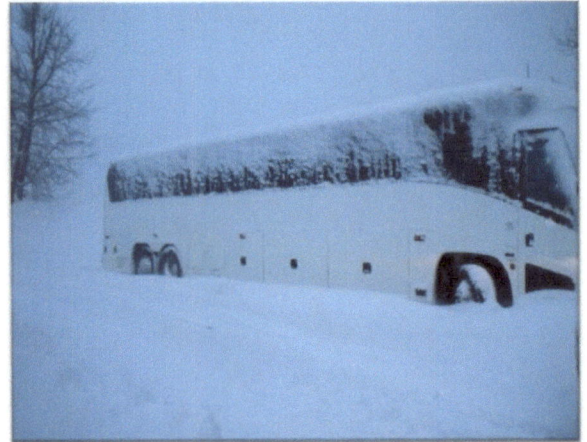

Valdez

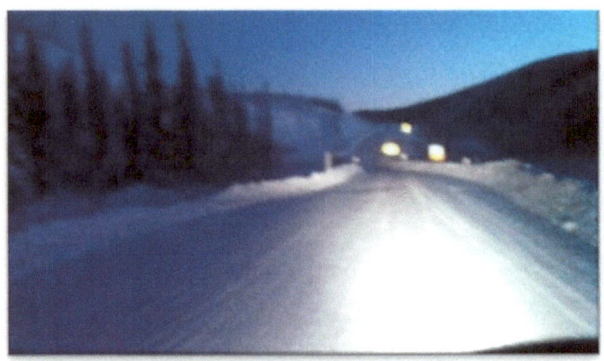

Above – 23 mile Pogo Mine Road – Delta (winter chain up)

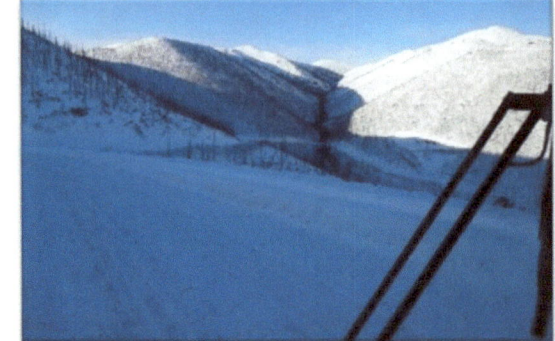

Dropping off the summit at 42 Mile

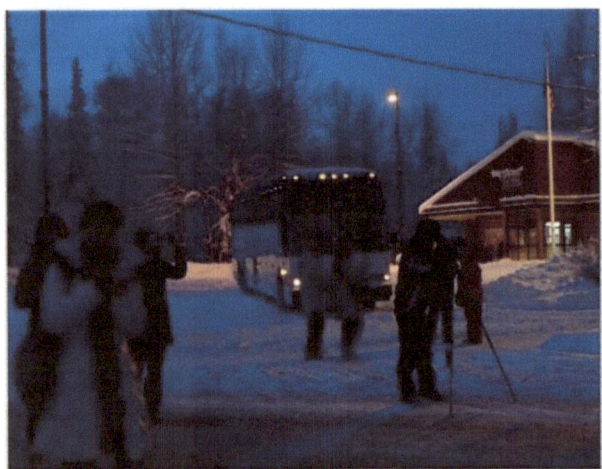

Talkeetna

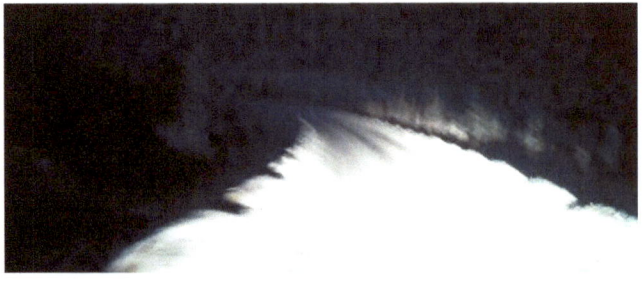

Chena Hot Springs Rd.

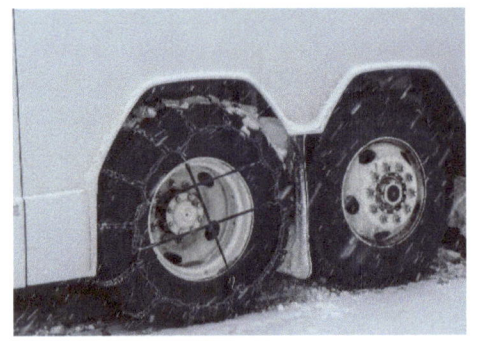

Winter Chain Up

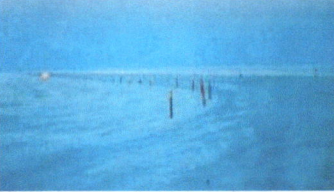

On the Beaufort Sea.

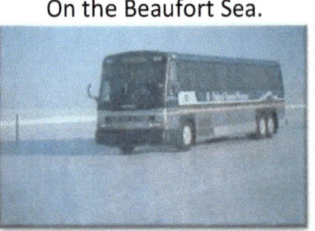

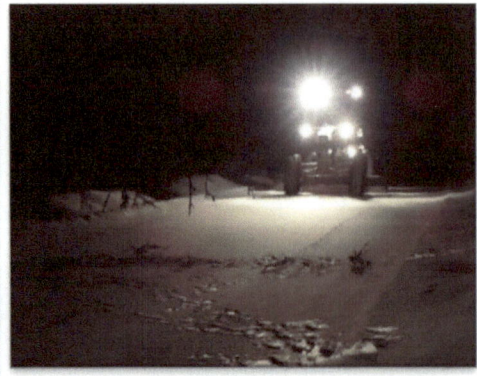

Wasilla Ididerod headquarters

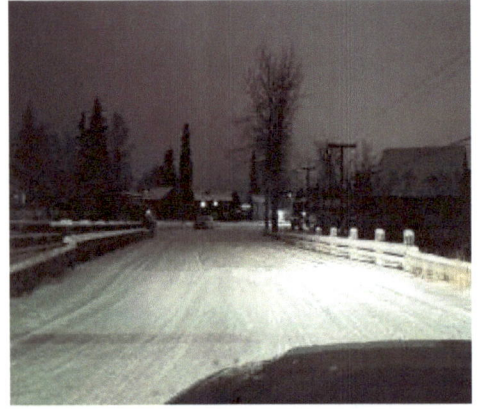

College, Alaska

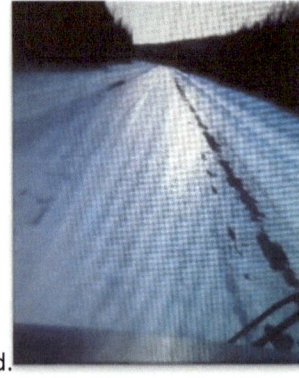

Chena Hot Springs Rd.

Tree across Pogo Mine Rd.

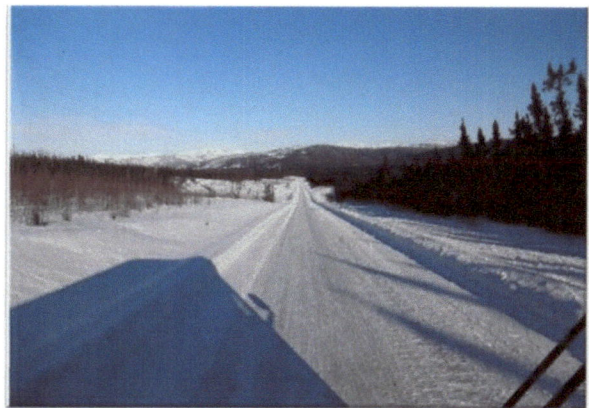
Pogo Rd.

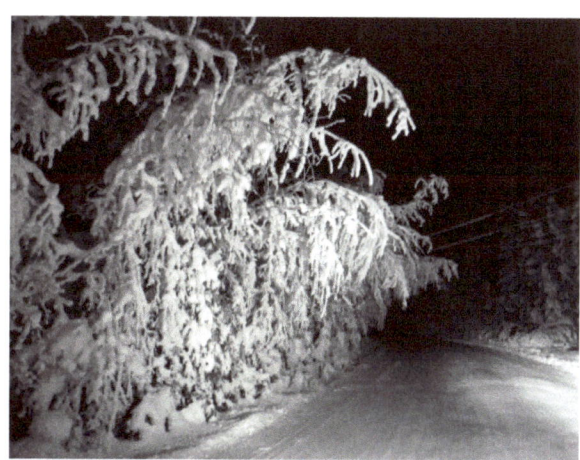
Off the Parks Hwy - Fairbanks

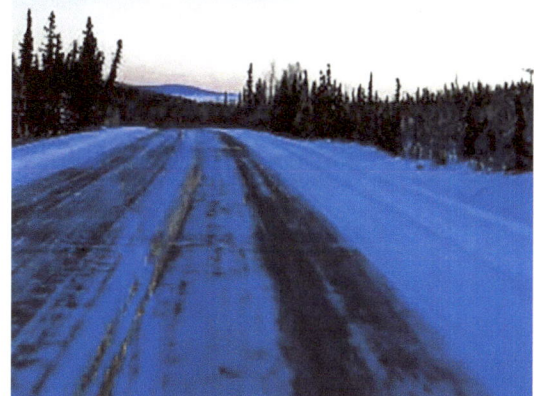
Chena Hot Springs Rd.

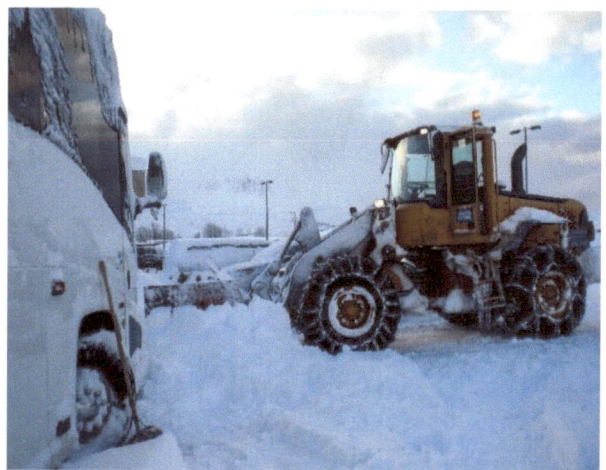
Stuck in Valdez

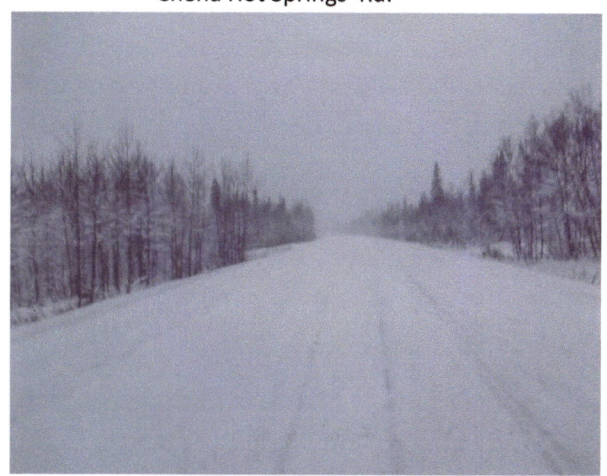
Parks Highway – south of Healy

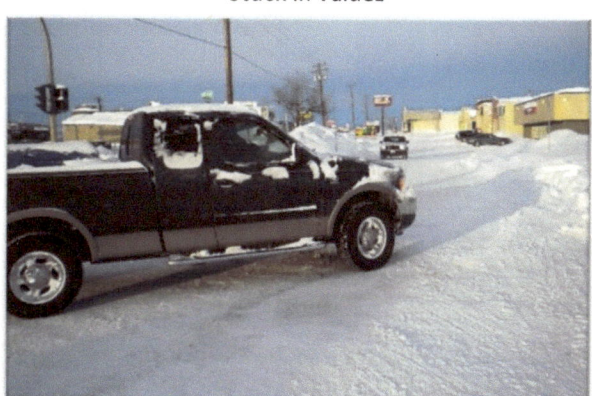
Yukon

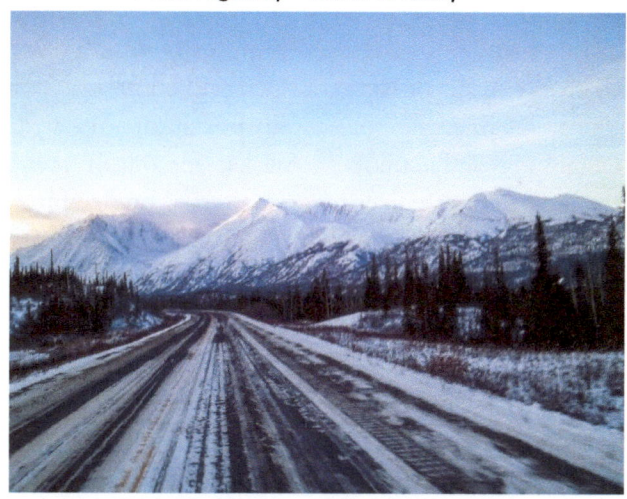
Parks Highway between Denali Park and Cantwell

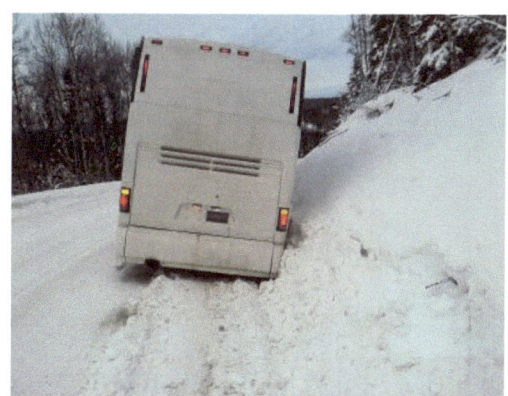
Moose Mountain Rd - Fairbanks

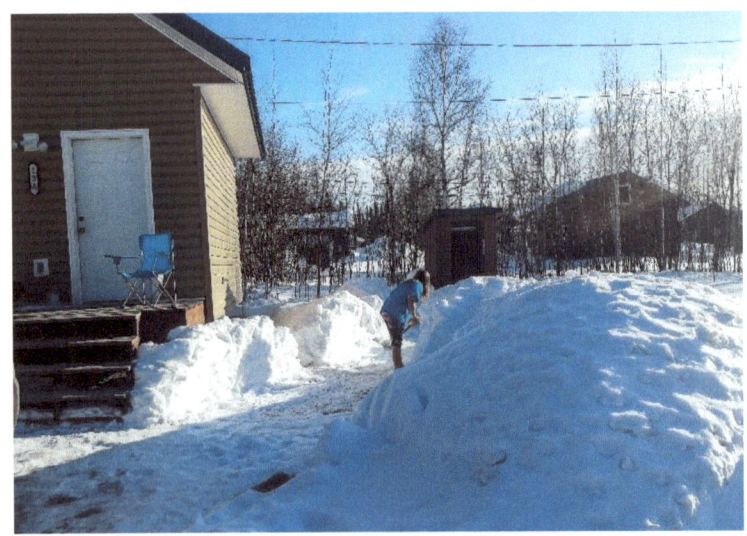
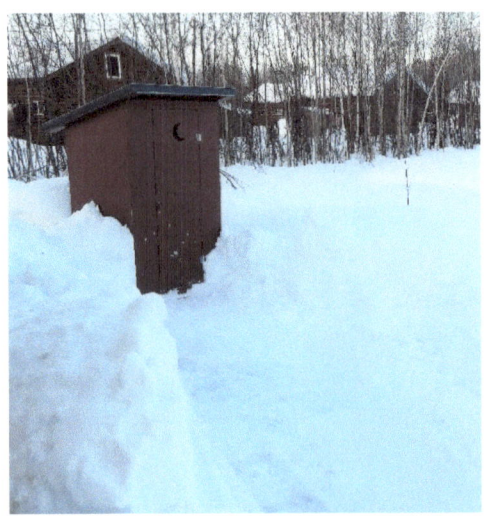

Life in a dry cabin means hauling water, taking a shower at a laundromat or the Rec. Center in town and keeping the path clear to the little house out back. During early pioneer days in America, the design on the door indicated men's or lady's – a star for men - the moon indicates a lady's room!

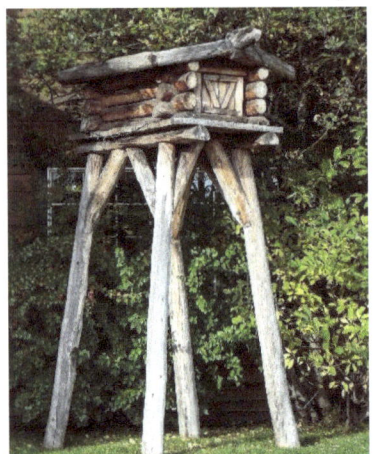

A cache kept supplies from animals during pioneer days. Tin wrapped around the lower end of the legs discouraged climbing. In winter, the cache became a freezer. Another cold storage method was a 55 gallon drum in the ground - permafrost remains frozen year-round and makes an excellent freezer. One side of the drum was opened, and shelves installed. Meat was put on lower shelves in order to remain frozen. Butter and milk went on top shelves where it would stay cold but not frozen. A lid was set on top to protect it from predators and keep the cold in. The drum was hauled up much the same way a bucket in a well was raised.

When the ice goes out on the Tanana River at Nenana, spring has officially arrived in the Interior of Alaska. A tripod is set up on the river; attached to shore by two ropes – one to a bell; the other to a clock. As the ice moves, the ropes tighten. The first rope releases the bell alerting the entire town that the river ice is going out. The second rope stops the clock – a matter of interest because a ticket can be purchased to guess the minute, the hour and the day clock stops.

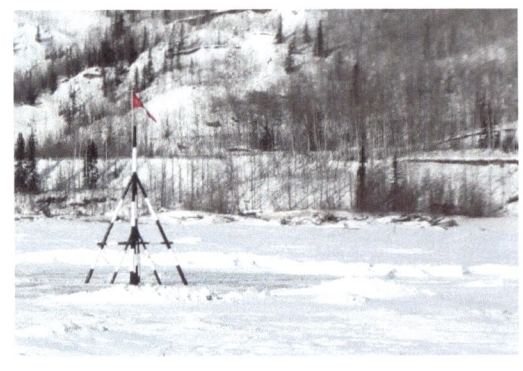

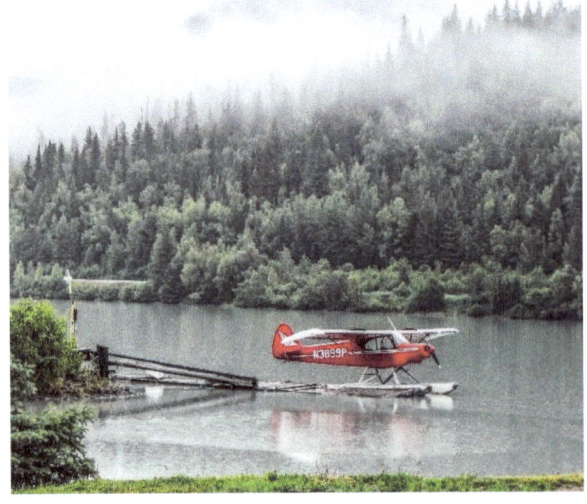

Because many of Alaska's remote communities are accessible only by air or water, air taxi and commuter planes are the only reliable year-round transportation. As of 2019, there were 8,288 active pilots in Alaska; one out of every 50 Alaskans has a pilot's license and aircraft ownership, per capita, is six times the national average. There are 394 public airports in the state – 109 of them seaplanes bases. Lake Hood, in Anchorage, is the world's largest and busiest seaplane base and the only seaplane base with primary airport status in the U.S. During 2018, there was a daily average of 200 landings and takeoffs with over 600 on peak summer days.

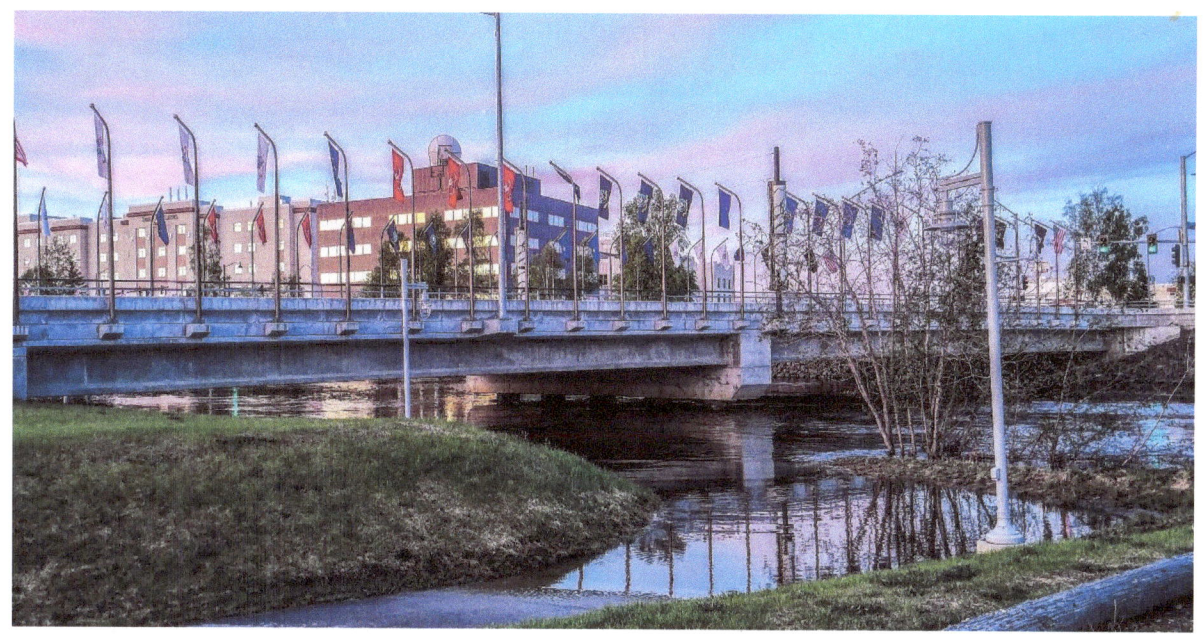

Fairbanks – May 27, 2018 - 3:41 a.m. – Chena River overflowing

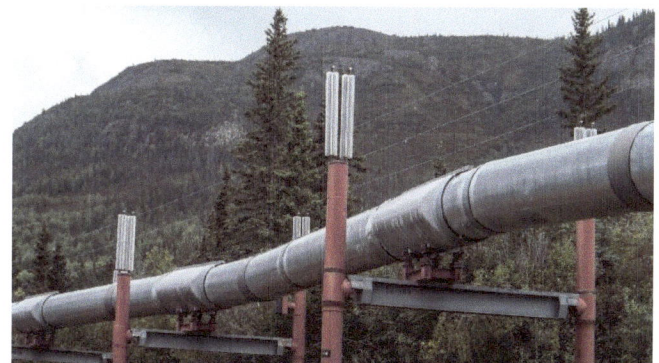

Fairbanks International Airport

TransAlaska Pipeline – Steese Hwy Fox, Alaska

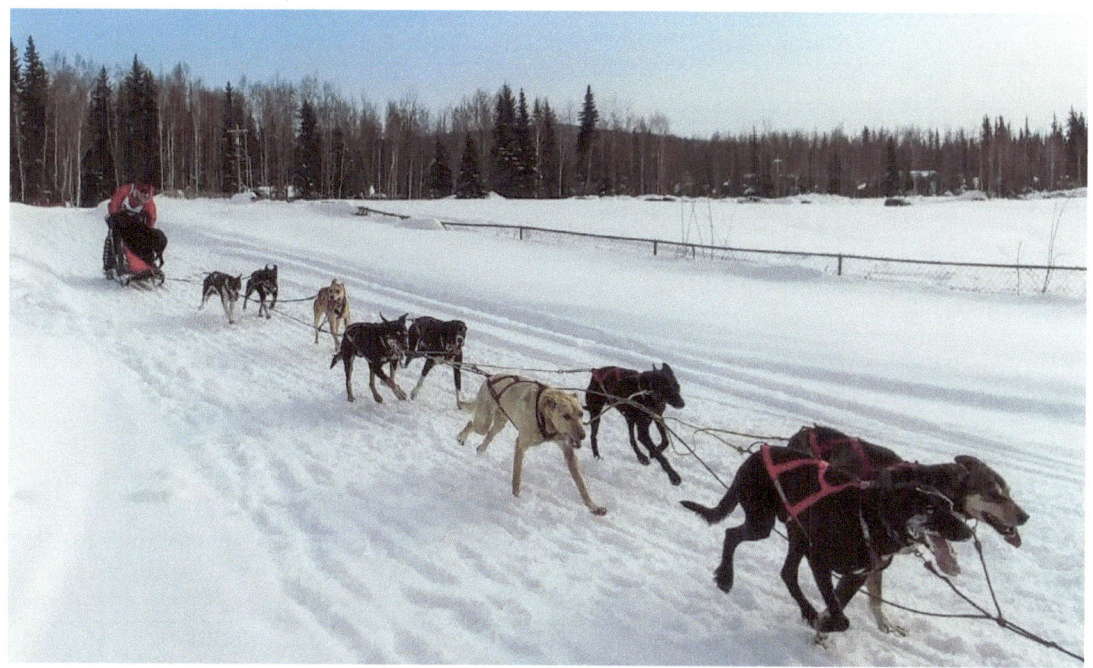

North American Sled Dog Race – Farmers Loop Road - Fairbanks

References

Alaska.Org – Bear Glacier

Alaska Dept. of Fish & Wildlife – Wood Bison

Alaska Dept. of Fish & Wildlife – Wolf

Alaska Dept. of Fish & Wildlife – Mountain Goat

Alaska Trekker – Alaska Bears

Anchorage Daily News - As Alaska Dall sheep populations shrink, guides and hunters vie for bigger share of harvest – Rick Sinnot - June 30, 2016

Bering Glacier – Alaska Dept. of Natural Resources

Bering Glacier, Alaska - NASA Earth Observatory

Coastview.org – Aialik Glacier, Kenai Fiords National Park - 4/26/2019

Exeter Symposium, July 1996 - Catastrophic discharge of fluvial sediment to the ocean: evidence of Jokulhlaups events in the Alsek Sea Valley, southeast Alaska (USA) - John D. Milliman, Jennifer Snow, John Jaeger, Charles A. Nittrouer

Glacier Hub – Photo Friday: Taku Glaciere is Finally Receding by Peter Deneen – Nov. 22, 2019

Global Warming Policy Forum – Alaska's Polar Bear Population Is Booming – Susan Crockford – Nov. 18, 2018

Interdisciplinary Science at the Bering Glacier - Michigan Tech Research Institute – 12/1/17

National Park Service – Alaska Nature & Science - July 15, 2019

Rainforest Adventures – The Amazon River - rfadventures.com

ReasearchGate – Canadian Journal of Earth Sciences - Neoglacial Lake Alsek - John J. Clague - February 2011

Springer Link – Prehistoric Archaeology on the Continental Shelf - Gateway to the Americas: Underwater Archeological Survey in Beringia and the North Pacific - James E. Dixon, Kelly Monteleone – May 6, 2014

University of Alaska Geophysical Institute - Gulkana Glacier buried while most of Alaska dry – Ned Rozell – 7/17/03

U.S. Dept. of Agriculture - Habitat of Steep Creek in Mendenhall Valley – The Juneau Icefield

U.S. Dept. of Agriculture – Forest Service – Portage Glacier & Portage Valley

The Conversation - First Americans lived on land bridge for thousands of years, genetics study suggests – 2/28/2014

What's the World's Biggest Glacier? By Karen Rowan - Live Science - June 10, 2010

Karen Simon moved to Fairbanks, Alaska in 1969. She has driven tour buses throughout Alaska and the Yukon for 20 years sharing the beauty, the history and stories of the land she has called home for over 50 years. The awe of the Northern Lights and the stunning beauty of the land inspired her to paint, with winter Aurora scenes and whales being her favorite subjects. This book rose out of the desire to share all seasons with visitors by creating a single photo album; but it was their enthusiasm for the book that prompted publishing.

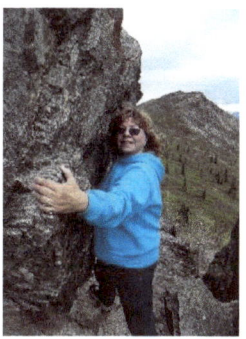

The author climbing rocks above
the Savage River in Denali Park

Other books by this author available at Amazon Books include

From Ranch to Rails

Crystal Cove

Discover Alaska

Yukon Memories

I Believe – Old Churches in Alaska & the Yukon

Washington State – Looking Back from Lava Flows to Statehood

Also available on Amazon and published by Alaska Dreams Publishing:

Inside the Circle

Ghost Cave Mountain

www.ingramcontent.com/pod-product-compliance
Lightning Source LLC
Chambersburg PA
CBHW050826180526
45159CB00004B/1800